I0814844

MAKE YOURSELF AT HOME

MAKE YOURSELF AT HOME

A Guide to Decorating with Heirlooms and Antiques that Tell Stories

CHELSEY BROWN

Gibbs Smith

To Mom, Dad, Mitch, Grandmay, and Papa

CONTENTS

Introduction

I STARTED MY CAREER AS A TV PRODUCER, obsessed with telling stories.

I then became an interior decorator and author, passionate about creating meaningful spaces in rented homes.

Next, I became an "heirloom hunter," finding and returning lost heirlooms to families.

For years, these parts of my life that felt so alienated from each other were actually the universe guiding me to this very moment. Writing this introduction is the moment I've realized I've come full circle, and that every passion and journey of mine was always meant to intertwine.

We live in a world where homes have become copies of carefully curated Pinterest boards and Instagram grids, and something profound has been lost. The very essence of what a home should be has faded into the background, overshadowed by the ecosystem of curated feeds and picture-perfect vignettes. In the wake of the pandemic of COVID-19 that shook up both 2020 and 2021 and gave many people more expendable time to browse the internet, and now amidst the frenzy of trying to imitate the lives, lifestyles, and design choices of influencers and celebrities we have thrown at us on a continual basis, we seem to have lost the true essence of what a home should be: *a story*.

Design is a form of art, right? Whether it's a painter's brush touching canvas, captured moments in a photograph, emotions conveyed in a movie, or the expressive movements in a dance, *ALL ART is meant to tell a story*. As a producer, and someone who loves storytelling, I am befuddled that designers have lost the heart and meaning behind what a home truly should be: a reflection and the story of the people living in it.

We so much want our homes to look like someone else's, that we've lost the soul, heart, and story of a home. Even designers have fallen prey, creating spaces that look pretty much identical to everyone else's.

Even with the most expensive furniture and top-tier interior designer, people are walking into their homes feeling like something is missing, and *no one can put a finger on it . . . until now*.

In 2021, my life took a captivating turn. While scouring flea markets for interior pieces, my heart would break every time I would come upon a box of family heirlooms. As my dad is a genealogist, I knew that many of these items weren't just being willingly discarded by families (more on that later).

These heirlooms were vessels of history, vessels that had stories to tell. It wasn't just the object that was fascinating: it was the story behind the item. Who did it belong to, what was their life story? What part did that object play in that person's life? Families had been unknowingly parted from these cherished treasures, and it became my mission to reunite them. The tears of joy, the overwhelming gratitude, and the newfound connections between generations as I handed over these heirlooms were moments that etched themselves into my soul.

And so, this book was conceived—a testament to the fusion of my multiple passions. It's a guide on how to decorate with antiques and family heirlooms, not as mere objects but as storytellers that breathe life into our living spaces.

Now we know that design is not just about aesthetics, but about storytelling. In this book, we will learn how to revive the lost art of creating homes that resonate with the lives they shelter, not by imitating the latest trends, but by *embracing the unique stories of the people who dwell within*.

HOW TO USE THIS BOOK

Designing with antiques while attempting to create a contemporary space is much harder than it looks, which is why you are probably reading this book! From go-to design formulas to easy-to-follow guidelines, this book is filled with everything you will need to know on how to *make yourself at home*.

However, I don't believe that just simply organizing this book by room (like many interior books you've seen before!) will do the information enough justice. So, before we dive into the fun stuff, let's go over how to best navigate these chapters, the way each section is organized, and some other important info.

The Sidebars

There's a lot of amazing text, and a lot of information to read and absorb. This is why you'll find sidebars with some can't-miss information.

PRO TIP

These are the most important tips and tricks that you won't want to miss!

BACKSTORY

Here I share the sentimental stories behind some of the beautiful pieces you see in this book.

WORK WITH WHAT YOU HAVE

If you know me, you know I love to find ways on how to transform a space without spending a dime. This sidebar teaches you how to work with items you already have in your space.

BEFORE YOU BUY

These are the tips you should follow before you swipe your card or add to your cart.

POINT OF VIEW

These are personal thoughts and beliefs based on my experience. Take them as guidelines for making design decisions that feel right for your space.

The Chapters

Instead of being organized by room, the chapters are organized by a series of guidelines and the size of items, offering a fresh perspective compared to the traditional room-by-room guide. We begin with the foundational knowledge and formulas needed to tackle sentimental items and spaces. From there, we navigate through strategies based on the size of these items, starting with larger antiques and moving toward smaller mementos. This structure aims to provide a clear and practical path for designing with and appreciating your treasured items. "All That Glitters Is Old: Sourcing Your Antiques" (page 133) will unlock secrets into flea markets, auctions, and online marketplaces as you find and acquire unique heirlooms and antique pieces. "Handle with Care: Preserving and Restoring Antiques" (page 155) will cover how to preserve, restore, and care for your treasured and sentimental pieces.

“NEW AND IMPROVED” IS HIGHLY OVERRATED

WHAT MAKES ANTIQUES, heirlooms, and vintage so captivating in this day and age? Is it the craftsmanship that outshines the mass-produced goods of today?

Or is it the historical significance that breathes life into every. single. detail. (All my fellow history nerds out there totally get this.)

Well, it’s partially that, but mostly the real answer lies in their *parallel stories*. In this chapter, we unravel the enduring appeal of these treasures in modern design.

Behind every chipped frame, faded letter, or that antique dining set is a tale worth telling. Many people forget that it's not just the actual heirloom, object, or piece of furniture that's important—**it's the story behind that item**, a story that could rival the most dramatic Hollywood script (Trust me, I've seen it firsthand).

Take, for instance, the weathered bookshelf, handed down through generations within your family, and that is now relegated to a back bedroom. That bookshelf may house your books and decorative accents now, but a hundred years ago, it whispered stories of countless bedtime tales, adventures, and maybe even a little *scandal*. In front of that bookshelf was where your grandmother told your grandfather he would be a parent. It's where your great-grandmother hid love letters from the boy she wasn't allowed to court.

It's more than just a "bookshelf."

What about that family photo album that has gradually meandered its way into a closet or basement? Well, a hundred years ago, that very photo album was your great-grandmother's passion project. She meticulously curated it, capturing every significant moment of her life, from wild adventures to secret rendezvous. And, oh boy, did it cause some family drama! Back then, her new boyfriend discovered an old flame's photo tucked away, setting off a whirlwind of emotions. Who knew that a photo album could be filled with such intrigue and romance?

You get the gist.

These objects possess an enchanting power to transport us to a different era, connecting us with our ancestors and reminding us of the rich tapestry of our family history. Even if it's an antique not necessarily passed down in your family, it still holds a story, a unique past, and however you acquired it now becomes part of its story.

BACKSTORY

In 2020, I thrifted a secretary desk from the late nineteenth century. You could clearly tell it had been heavily used for over a century, with the marks engraved in its wood and the wear you could see within the drawers.

This desk is where I wrote my second book. It's also where I designed my first ever product in my business. These incredible and powerful moments make me wonder about the similarly impactful memories a previous owner might have had with this desk.

Maybe love letters were once written here. Or maybe someone's divorce was finalized at this desk. I think about how, similar to me, laughter, smiles, and even tears were also shed over the same wood I am writing on now.

And let's take a step back and think even smaller: Imagine stumbling upon a vintage camera at a flea market—a relic from the past that captured moments of joy and laughter. Every single click of the shutter revealed a story, frozen in time, filled with adventures, love, and maybe even a little mischief.

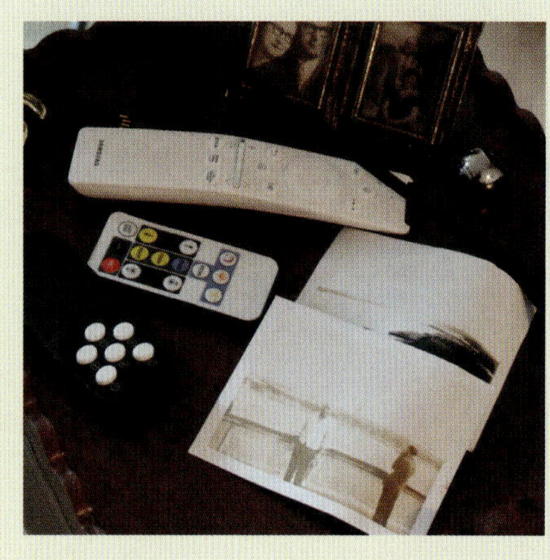

BACKSTORY

I happened to find an old film camera from the 1960s at a flea market in New York City. When I brought it home, a photo slipped out of the beaten camera bag. It was a photo of the original owner holding this exact camera. I keep this photo and film camera displayed in my living room.

In a world that's always searching for the next big thing, it's essential to preserve these heirlooms and antiques. In fact, I think that's partially why antiques and vintage finds are coming back in style. In this digital age, we are craving that old-world charm and details you just don't see anymore.

These treasures, antiques, and vintage pieces possess an undeniable charm that enhance and create character within any contemporary design (which is obviously what this book is about!). Picture an old-timey gramophone displayed proudly amidst sleek, contemporary furniture, or an intricately embroidered quilt adorning a minimalist bedroom. The fusion of old and new creates a drool-worthy juxtaposition, infusing spaces with character and charm that just makes it feel homey.

WORK WITH WHAT YOU HAVE

Imagine running your fingers across the delicate engravings of a silver pocket watch, imagining the moments it witnessed—a wedding ceremony, a soldier's brave departure, or a cherished reunion. Each scratch and mark tells a story, a chapter of history waiting to be discovered. This watch can be displayed on your dresser in a tray, acting not only as a mini time capsule to the past but as a unique decorative statement.

PRO TIP

Furniture pieces made in the eighteenth, nineteenth, and twentieth centuries often stand out for their superior craftsmanship and unique character compared to the mass-produced furniture made today.

AGED LIKE FINE WINE AND BUILT TO LAST

Craftsmanship is often another integral part of some of these treasures. The exquisite attention to detail and the hours of labor poured into creating certain pieces speak of a bygone era when quality and artistry were paramount (think eighteenth-, nineteenth-, and twentieth-century furniture). These items, imbued with the hands of skilled artisans, stand as testaments to the beauty of human craftsmanship. Something you rarely see in home and furniture design nowadays.

There are several reasons why this is the case.

Attention to Detail. The artisans of furniture (of the past) paid meticulous attention to detail, taking the time to carefully handcraft each piece. Every joint, carving, and embellishment was crafted with precision, resulting in furniture that exuded a sense of quality and artistry. This level of craftsmanship was a reflection of the pride and skill that went into creating each piece.

For example, just the basic construction of a nineteenth-century dining table versus now is noncomparable. An intricately carved eighteenth-century wooden dining table might feature not only amazing design, but also dense, well-aged wood that has darkened and looks almost raw in certain places. In addition, the joints, crafted with precision, were often dovetail or mortise and tenon, showcasing the artistry of the time.

You can learn how to identify the age of furniture on **page 136**.

Quality Materials. In the past, furniture was commonly made from high-quality, solid wood such as mahogany, oak, or walnut. These durable materials were carefully selected for their strength and beauty, ensuring that the furniture would stand the test of time.

Unique Designs. Furniture from the nineteenth and twentieth centuries often featured distinctive designs and aesthetics that reflected the artistic movements of the time. From the elegant curves of art nouveau to the clean lines of art deco, these furniture styles showcased creativity, individuality, and oh-so-much character.

Handcrafted Techniques. Skilled artisans of the past employed traditional handcrafted techniques, such as hand-carving, joinery, and marquetry, to create intricate and visually appealing details. These techniques required a high level of expertise and added an element of artistry to the furniture.

Patina and Aging. Over time, furniture from the past develops a unique patina and character that adds to its charm and appeal. The natural wear, scratches, and signs of aging tell a story and give the furniture a sense of history and authenticity. Natural wood loses its shine over time.

The catch-22? We live in a world where there is modern, contemporary furniture with fantastic craftsmanship, but most of it is unattainable to the average consumer. Therefore, most of us DO need to mix and match those mass-produced products with antique treasures.

BEFORE YOU BUY

Ok, I get it: Mass-produced furniture offers affordability and convenience, but again, it often falls short in terms of craftsmanship and character. Furniture from nineteenth- and twentieth-centuries artisans, with its attention to detail, quality materials, unique designs, handcrafted techniques, and aged patina, continues to captivate and stand out as a testament to the enduring beauty of traditional craftsmanship.

POINT OF VIEW

You may know this, but this is why older pre-war homes are rising in popularity. Lack of architectural detail and builder-grade homes are not for everyone. There can be a lot of character and charm in buildings built pre-1950s.

PRESERVING THE PAST

But how do we persuade both older and younger generations to resist the urge to discard antiques or sentimental items or to try and cover them up? It KILLS me when I see "furniture flippers" stripping and painting over beautiful wood. These types of "antiques" are only going to make your home feel unbalanced. I see this all the time, not just in my personal life and with previous clients but also on social media.

Again, it starts with understanding and appreciating the deep-rooted emotions attached to them. The worn-out armchair might not look like much to an outsider, but for your grandparents, it was a symbol of countless cozy evenings spent with loved ones.

Plus, we now know that unless you can afford high-quality, modern craftsmanship, these antiques are the closest thing you're going to get to pure artistry.

In a world obsessed with the latest trends and disposable culture, there's something rebellious and empowering about holding onto our heirlooms and antiques, right?

Most important, as someone who returns lost heirlooms to families, one of the biggest regrets I hear families discuss is the discarding of furniture. Usually, parents or grandparents will ask the next generations if they want anything. The kids and grandkids say no, and five or ten years later those younger generations have deep regrets.

In fact, this happened to me. When I was a teenager, my mom asked me if I wanted my grandmother's dresser, and I said, "Eww, no." To this day I regret losing that item. I hope whoever has it now is taking good care of it.

Throughout this book, I'll be sharing some of my favorite antique finds and family heirlooms and telling the movie-esque stories behind them.

POINT OF VIEW

Contrary to popular belief, families don't willingly throw away family heirlooms. Most of the heirlooms and artifacts I acquire to return to families end up in my hands due to family drama. For example, a family member gets access to an estate and instead of giving belongings to family members, the entire estate is sold off for a quick buck.

If you're not quite ready to invest in a large or pricey antique piece, start small by pairing an antique art print with a vintage frame. This one vintage piece in this bathroom ends up being an entire statement of its own.

TALE AS OLD AS ~~TIME~~ PRIME

It's quite fitting that Mrs. Potts was the one to sing "Tale as Old as Time," because even the smallest of objects can tell the most magnificent tales, even a chipped teacup.

We need to resist the temptation to discard these sentimental pieces and instead embrace the emotional ties and historical narratives they represent. By valuing and preserving vintage heirlooms and antiques, we not only ensure that their stories endure (I should write lullabies), but we create homes that tell a story of the person/people living inside of it. We're designing unique spaces that *feel something* and don't just look like every other home you see on social media.

So, it's ok to buy that coffee table from Amazon, or the office desk from Wayfair or IKEA. But don't discard the furniture and items passed down from previous generations, or don't pass up on that vintage find at your local flea market because you **can make them work,** and I'll show you how!

BEFORE YOU DESIGN, LET'S DEFINE

What's in Your Collection?

THERE'S A REASON why your home might not feel quite right, despite the constant stream of new decor from Target or HomeGoods. You're following trends, picking up pieces you think will make your space feel luxurious, but instead, it's coming off as generic or cutesy rather than unique. The problem is you're curating your home, not truly collecting for it. You're copying what you see on Pinterest and Instagram instead of gathering items that have personal meaning and speak to you. This shift in mindset—from curating to collecting—can be transformative.

To start, clear your mind of the idea that you need to keep buying decor. Instead, look around and work with what you already own—especially items that have been passed down through your family. In today's world, craftsmanship is increasingly rare, and many of the mass-produced items we buy don't hold a candle to pieces made decades ago. When I work with clients, I always begin by "shopping" their own homes, rediscovering hidden treasures they've stored away because they thought the pieces weren't trendy enough. These older, well-crafted items often carry more character and quality than anything you can find on store shelves today. Likewise, when you do shop at antique malls or flea markets, choose objects that resonate with you on a personal level, rather than copying the aesthetics you see online. Collect what speaks to you—don't just curate what looks like it belongs in someone else's feed.

Before we get into the fun of designing, we first need to assess your collection of heirlooms, vintage items, and antiques to know what we're working with. In this chapter, I'll help you identify what those pieces are.

OPPOSITE: Looking for something different for your walls, or do you have a collection of old handbags or jewelry you no longer wear? Including different types of objects in a wall display makes a unique statement. LEFT: Not everything needs a frame. Layering an oil painting on canvas over metal chains can give your room a really cool vibe.

THE DIFFERENCE BETWEEN ANTIQUES, VINTAGE, MEMENTOS, AND FAMILY HEIRLOOMS

Antiques, mementos, and family heirlooms are all objects that hold significance and value, but they differ in their origin, purpose, and emotional attachment. Let's get the terminology out of the way.

Antiques

Antiques are items that are old, typically over a century in age, and possess historical, cultural, or artistic value. They often have distinct craftsmanship and are considered collectibles. The appeal of antiques lies in their ability to connect us with different eras and offer a glimpse into the past. Here are a few examples.

- **An eighteenth-century Chippendale chair. A beautifully crafted wooden chair with intricate carvings and exceptional craftsmanship. It is highly sought after by collectors and enthusiasts of antique furniture.**
- **An antique French armoire. A tall, freestanding wardrobe with intricate carvings and a mirrored door, originating from France in the eighteenth century.**
- **An antique oil painting. A masterpiece painted by a renowned artist from a specific art movement or era, such as an impressionist or baroque painting.**

If you gravitate toward more antiques and fewer contemporary pieces but still want your space to feel modern, matching tones and patterns is key. Incorporating florals, fabrics, and art with similar undertones will naturally create a modern aesthetic without needing anything physically modern in the room at all.

Antiques often hold monetary value and can appreciate over time, making them investments for collectors. They are admired for their aesthetic appeal, historical significance, and the stories they might carry. But antiques might not be the most important of your family's history.

Vintage Items

The term "vintage" refers to items that, while not as old as antiques, usually fall between twenty to ninety-nine years old. These items are appreciated for their representation of the style and trends of a particular era rather than their age alone. Their collectibility and value are tied more to their visual appeal and the specific historical period they represent. Many people use the term "vintage" and "antique" interchangeably. Two samples of vintage items are mentioned below.

- A Pierre Paulin pumpkin chair. First designed in 1971, this chair is instantly recognizable for its organic, rounded form that resembles a pumpkin, lending it both its name and distinctive look. The playful round shape captures the essence of the time. (Fun fact: this was when design boundaries were being pushed toward more radical and expressive forms.) The chair that's shown here is a reissue of the design by the Paulin estate called "Alpha."
- A bullnose dresser. This type of furniture from the 1980s is a quintessential piece of the era, merging more modern materials with a nod to traditional design. Its defining feature is obviously the rounded bullnose edges of the drawers. Often made with a mix of laminates or wood, it represents the 1980s eclectic style—a blend of minimalism and curved details.

Not sure which vintage or antique style feels right for you yet? Turn your TV into a temporary art piece with a YouTube screensaver. It gives the look of curated art, isn't a permanent choice, and lets you switch it up anytime while you figure out your style.

ADAM STYLE
TAMSIN JOHNSON

HOUSE&GARDEN
TAMSIN JOHNSON Spaces for Living

Mementos

Mementos are objects that serve as reminders of specific events, places, or people. They are chosen and kept for sentimental reasons, preserving memories and emotions. Mementos may not be old or valuable in a traditional sense, but they hold immense personal significance. You know what is important to you, but here are two examples.

- **Concert ticket stubs. Ticket stubs from a favorite band's concert, kept as a reminder of an amazing night with friends.**
- **Photographs. Family photo albums or individual photos that captured certain life memories.**

Mementos can vary greatly in form and material, but their value is rooted in the emotions and memories they represent. They are way too often stored away in a closet or drawer.

Mementos aren't necessarily meant to be tucked away in drawers or memory boxes. Frame your favorite letters from your favorite people in modern frames. It's such a beautiful way to create a one-of-a-kind art piece that's all about you and your story.

Family Heirlooms

Family heirlooms are possessions, often with high sentimental value, that are passed down from one generation to another. These items can include all of the above (antiques, vintage items, or mementos), jewelry, furniture, letters, diaries, or even clothing. The essence of family heirlooms lies in their role as connectors between generations, carrying forward the history and legacy of a family. Have you been bequeathed any of these?

- **Your grandfather's wedding ring. An antique gold ring passed down through several generations.**
- **A handmade quilt. A quilt lovingly crafted by a great-grandparent.**
- **Your grandmother's travel diary. A weathered leather-bound diary filled with handwritten notes, sketches, and/or mementos from your grandmother's travels around the world.**

Family heirlooms can hold sentimental rather than monetary value, contrary to popular belief. As cheesy as this sounds, the act of passing down antiques, vintage items, mementos, and heirlooms fosters a sense of continuity and connection between generations.

While they may differ in age, value, and purpose, all four categories of objects contribute to the rich tapestry of our interiors and homes.

PRO TIP

If you take away only one thing from this book, it should be this. Whether your family heirlooms are in your home, or your parents' home, maybe even with your grandparents, you need to ask, NOW, the importance behind each item, who it first belonged to, and its significance. This includes any mementos saved within the family. And write that information down so it is available to whoever will inherit the treasure. Don't wait until it's too late to ask questions about certain items. Ask. Those. Questions. Now.

If you're just starting out collecting, I recommend beginning with antique vases. The craftsmanship of older pieces like the one on this table is often far superior to anything you'll find new today!

A MATCH MADE IN HISTORY

Mixing Old and New

MODERN AND CONTEMPORARY might sound like the same thing—but in the interior world, they have totally different meanings.

Modern design refers to a specific design movement that emerged in the early to mid-twentieth century. It's characterized by clean lines, minimalism, and functionality. Modern design is timeless; it doesn't adhere to come-and-go trends but is rooted in a particular era's design philosophy. It also often features geometric shapes. Furniture and architectural elements are typically sleek and angular, contributing to a sense of order and simplicity.

On the other hand, contemporary design became popular in the 1970s, about the same time as postmodernism's rise in popularity. It was originally a blend of styles before it became recognizable as its own interior style. Contemporary design basically borrowed elements from modernism and postmodernism, while also taking inspiration from many other styles such as art deco, deconstructivism, futurism, and more.

What Is "Trendy"

Subject to Change. Being trendy means following the latest fads in design (whether that be in fashion or interiors). Trends come and go, and what's fashionable today may be outdated tomorrow. Trendiness is inherently changeable—and it's risky to design your home with trends, especially when on a budget.

Surface-Level Aesthetics. Trends often focus on surface-level aesthetics, such as color schemes, patterns, and decor styles. They may not necessarily consider functionality or long-term practicality, which is a big deal when it comes to well-made pieces. Trends may not prioritize timeless design principles.

Inauthentic. Trends are heavily influenced by pop culture, media, and the opinions of influencers. They are driven by what's currently popular rather than personal taste, which means your home may end up looking like someone else's Pinterest board rather than a reflection of yourself.

Short-Lived. Trends have a relatively short lifespan. What's considered trendy at the moment may quickly lose its appeal as new trends emerge. This can really hurt your bank account if you are always purchasing the latest decor.

But here's what's really important: The "contemporary" style is always changing. As each decade passes, the decor trends of the day will always be considered *contemporary*. It is not tied to a specific time period the way modern style is. Instead, it is an ever-evolving style that reflects what is happening today.

Now, let's get this out of the way: Contemporary design and being trendy are also completely different ideas. (Although many Pinterest boards and TikTok feeds would make you think otherwise.) This book is about how to seamlessly integrate antique with the contemporary, but I've tried very hard to avoid the "trendy."

Ok, so what do you really need to know? Contemporary design stands the test of time and remains relevant *regardless of changing trends*. While contemporary design can incorporate elements of trendiness, it is ultimately a design philosophy with its own identity. Design enthusiasts (like us!) often strike a balance between the two, incorporating trendy elements and antique pieces into a contemporary or timeless foundation.

If you're more drawn to vintage than antique and want to make a statement, combining wood and metal is always a reliable, fail-safe choice.

I love when people bring a whimsical touch to contemporary-meets-old spaces. If you want to lean into that luxurious vibe, canopies are an amazing option (and they're not just for the bedroom.

THE RULE OF PAIRS

Creating an interior that marries the past with the present is pretty much like conducting a symphony. It requires an understanding of composition and balance. One of the *main* key techniques we'll explore is the "Rule of Pairs." This rule is all about creating a balanced narrative within your space, and it's how you'll be able to mix countless interior styles and eras into your space.

The rule of pairs is simple. Basically, you complement whatever piece you are trying to incorporate in your space with a similar texture and color in the same room. Here are a few examples for context.

Imagine you have an antique mahogany secretary desk. It's a statement, a conversation starter, but everything else in the room is neutral-contemporary. The secretary desk just feels out of place, but you can't put your finger on why.

This is where the rule of pairs comes into play. Seek out another item that shares a similar texture and color with that secretary desk and weave a common thread through the room. Perhaps it's a set of mahogany frames for an art piece, or a vintage chair with mahogany legs that now has its place. This simple, yet powerful rule creates symmetry and cohesiveness, allowing you to incorporate as many antiques as your heart desires without overwhelming the space!

The two main things to remember with the rule of pairs: First, you need to make sure the "pair" is not placed right next to the existing item. First, you need to make sure the pair is not placed right next to the existing item. It needs to be placed across the room (this can also be a diagonal cross) or with a contrasting piece of furniture in between. Second, the two objects in the pair need to be the same color and texture.

The great thing about the rule of pairs is that once you have a pair in a space, you can start adding items in the same room with similar color and texture. I am constantly doing this with different wood tones. And you can mix woods (unless they have different undertones!)

The small antique stool pairs perfectly with the antique secretary desk. Their matching color and texture tie together, while a modern chair in between adds contrast.

THE ART OF JUXTAPOSITION

In addition to the rule of pairs, one of the most enchanting aspects of mixing old and new is the dynamic interplay between contrasting elements. When done thoughtfully, these juxtapositions can elevate your space from ordinary to extraordinary.

Juxtapositions will happen between antique and contemporary items and will play off colors, patterns, and shapes.

For example, imagine a living room where a sleek, white, cloud-like sofa takes center stage. At its feet lies a traditional Persian rug, rich in intricate patterns. The contrast is striking, and it's precisely this juxtaposition that adds depth and character to the room. The cool, smooth contours of the sofa are balanced by the warmth and complexity of the rug, creating a visual symphony that is both captivating and comforting. This is an example of using a juxtaposition with color and pattern.

You can also incorporate juxtapositions in your space with antiques using shapes. Place a curved, modern mirror over a nineteenth-century antique wood buffet, for example.

You can effortlessly mix and match vintage and antique pieces. Here, the vintage sofa is a stylish counterpoint to the antique chest of drawers.

THE ART OF MISMATCHING

When it comes to objects in a similar realm and close together in a space, antiques of different styles can be easily placed together. Think of things like art, dining chairs, living room chairs, and decor.

Consider a dining area where a table shares the spotlight with a collection of random antique chairs. Each chair has its history, whether passed down through generations or discovered in a dusty antique shop.

Or imagine a gallery wall with mismatched antique frames and artwork. It may seem incongruous at first, but when they are antiques, it feels purposeful. I much prefer these types of gallery walls versus ones where the frames look alike or are perfectly matched. I love the character it brings to the wall.

The frames and art pieces in this space are completely mismatched, but together they make a cool statement wall.

THE FORMULA FOR SUCCESS

It's time to do a little math! Just kidding . . . but not really. Creating a seamless integration between antique and contemporary pieces requires careful consideration and a dash of creativity. Here's a fail-proof formula if you're starting from scratch.

Start with a focal point. Select a focal point for the room, whether it's an antique piece, a piece of artwork, or a striking modern element. This focal point will serve as the anchor for your design.

Maintain a cohesive color palette. Choose a color palette that unifies the vintage and modern elements. This could involve repeating a specific color or using complementary hues that tie everything together. Personally, I like using complementary hues first and then incorporating fun colors in my antique art and florals.

Balance Proportions. Ensure that the scale and proportions of the objects in the room are harmonious. Don't keep everything the same height! Mix and match taller objects with shorter ones while also mixing and matching furniture with open and closed bottoms.

PRO TIP

When you're aiming to create a contemporary space while incorporating antiques, I always recommend keeping your window treatments modern. Sleek blinds, minimalist shades, or simple curtains can help balance the vintage charm of your antiques and keep the overall look fresh and updated.

However, if your space already has a majority of contemporary pieces, feel free to experiment with more traditional curtains or window treatments. This can add a touch of elegance and complement your antiques without overwhelming the modern aesthetic. The key is to maintain a balance that highlights both the old and the new.

The cool-toned tapestry draped over the banquette ties in with the cool hues of the floors and walls. Modern velvet pillows add a contemporary touch, making the space feel dynamic.

DON'T FORGET THE MODERN

I know this book is about decorating with antiques and vintage, but to create a contemporary home, we must incorporate our antiques with contemporary furniture. We've now got the rule of pairs, juxtaposition, and mismatching down, which is a huge help, but there's a BIG topic we gotta get out of the way right now. And the furniture stores won't like me for this one!

Let's use a real-life scenario, shall we? You've just walked by the most stunning piece of furniture at Crate & Barrel. It's got cloudy-dreamy-funky (did I catch them all?) vibe you've been drooling over on Instagram. It's picture perfect, and you need it RIGHT. NOW.

Ok, well, hold up a sec. Let's discuss.

First off, props to the store and their employees. They know exactly how to light, accessorize, and style that piece of furniture so it looks straight out of a magazine spread. You walk in, and bam, you're convinced this one item is going to change your life, or at the very least, your living room. It's a well-played illusion.

But here's the tea. Plucking that gorgeous piece and plopping it into your own space doesn't guarantee the same effect. That trendy store? They've got professionals who painstakingly set up everything to look just so. Your home, on the other hand, is a unique space with its own challenges, dimensions, and existing decor.

Many of us have been there. We buy that swoon-worthy piece, hoping it's the missing puzzle to our dream home. But then, once it's in our space, something feels . . . off. It's not the furniture's fault. It's just that creating a cohesive, beautiful space isn't about that one piece, no matter how gorgeous. It's about how everything interacts—the harmony of the furniture with the space, other pieces, and even the light.

So, before you dive wallet-first into that purchase, take a step back. Consider the bigger picture of your space. How will it fit in? How will you style it? Will it compete or complement?

In the end, the key isn't in buying the trendiest pieces, but in understanding your own space and needs. Sometimes, it's about rearranging, decluttering, or simply adding a new throw or a lamp. The beauty is in the balance and how you bring everything together. This is why I suggest always assessing your collection of antiques first to get a better idea of the types of contemporary accents you'll need to either pair or juxtapose with.

PRO TIP

Pay attention to lighting. Another go-to rule for me is to keep the lighting fixtures in a room within the same time period. For example, if you have a modern or contemporary floor lamp, make sure the other table lamps and lights in the space are also contemporary.

Looking for a statement feature that not many other people have? Try mounting your TV on an antique easel. Not only is it a fun look, it's functional. Your guests will your guests notice it every time they step into your home.

This is a superb example of pairing smaller antiques with modern elements. The disco ball layered over the antique ladder, or a sleek modern vase placed next to antique book creates a contrast that feels intentional.

BEFORE YOU BUY

Ok, here's my number one rule for purchasing items. I NEVER buy a piece of furniture, whether contemporary or antique, without creating a mood board or seeing how it looks in my space first.

There are two ways to do this: You can either create a mood board or simply photoshop an item into a photo of your space.

A mood board is essentially a visual tool that combines visuals to convey a specific style, concept, or mood. It's often used in interior design, fashion, and branding, which is why you've probably heard it referred to within a creative setting! Mood boards basically help to clarify a vision and ensure that everyone involved in a project is on the same page regarding the look and feel.

For creating mood boards, Pinterest and Canva are my go-to platforms of choice.

> **Pinterest.** This platform is fantastic for gathering inspiration and organizing it into boards. You can easily save images, patterns, and ideas from all over the web and categorize them.
>
> **Canva.** Canva offers more structured mood board creation tools, allowing you to upload your own images and use templates to arrange your visuals neatly. It's perfect for more polished presentations, where you can add text, shapes, and various design elements to really define the mood or concept you're presenting.

My recommendation is that when buying contemporary, if you photoshop the item into a picture of your space and you're not loving the outcome, don't buy it. However, if you photoshop a vintage or antique item into your space and you are 50/50, I suggest buying the item. Why? For me it's better to buy and resell than not buy and regret!!

Remember, your home is your canvas. And while that trendy piece might be a fabulous brushstroke, it's how you paint the whole picture that truly makes it a masterpiece. Plopping in a piece you love, whether contemporary or antique, isn't going to magically transform that room. You need to use the rule of pairs, juxtapositions, mismatching, and contrasting to make all of the items work together.

THE BIG, BOLD, AND BEAUTIFUL

Decorating with Larger Antique Furniture

THIS IS WHERE THE FUN STARTS! Now that we've got the nitty-gritty rules and guidelines down, let's start working those beautiful vintage and antique pieces into your home. We will start with larger items and gradually make our way to smaller items throughout the chapters.

When either designing a space from scratch or working with what you have, I use the rule of "bases" to help bring a space together. Your bases are your large furniture items—sofa, bed, cabinets, and other big-ticket pieces. These are your splurge-worthy investments, both in size and budget. Since they dominate the space, use them as your design anchors. Think of them as the foundation for your redesign masterpiece.

SIZE DOES MATTER: WHAT IS CONSIDERED A LARGE ANTIQUE PIECE

A large furniture piece is generally something that you can't transport in the back of your car. It might require delivery, special handling with furniture padding, and maybe some reassembly after it arrives. If you are working with any of the below items, you are technically working with a large antique piece.

- **Armoires or wardrobes**
- **Buffets, sideboards, and credenzas**
- **Canopy beds and four-poster beds**
- **Most coffee tables**
- **Chests of drawers, dressers, and highboys**
- **Dining tables (including extendable and drop-leaf tables)**
- **Bookcases and library cabinets; some étagères**
- **Writing desks and secretaires (wider than 45 inches)**
- **Sofas (over 77 inches wide)**
- **Display cabinets and china hutches**
- **Large musical instruments: think pianos, organs, harps**

Different wood tones can pair well as long as they have the same undertone. The antique chest of drawers and modern wood box have a warm undertone. OVERLEAF: Furniture doesn't always have to serve its original purpose. This antique secretary desk, for example, is repurposed as a bar cabinet. The modern glassware nicely elevates and complements the look of this piece.

WORKING AROUND AN ANTIQUE PIECE VERSUS WORKING IT IN

Let's start with working around. The first thing to focus on is the rule of pairs. This example will pretty much work for any large piece, but let's say you have a beautiful antique kitchen island. Here's how to make everything else play nice with it.

Let her be the leading lady. Your antique is the boss. Let it set the tone for all the other items you choose. Think of it as the main character in your story, with all the other furniture as supporting cast.

Complement, don't compete. Find a few modern pieces that share a little something with your antique—maybe it's a touch of gold or the curve of a leg. This way, your old treasure and new finds feel like they're on the same team.

Light it right. Good lighting can make your antique sing. A sleek, modern lamp beside an old wooden desk can highlight its best features without overpowering it.

Space it out. Give your antique some breathing room. Don't crowd it with too much stuff. A little space lets it stand out and tells everyone, "Hey, look at this amazing piece!"

To bridge the gap between the antique and the room, introduce some large frames that mimic the rich tone of the wood. The shared color palette and texture weave a thread of continuity, while the differing items and aged wood play off each other, creating a look that's cohesive and *intentional*.

PRO TIP

Just inherited or thrifted an antique chair or sofa, but it isn't comfortable? Try ordering new cushions or foam inserts to make that piece feel brand new again!

Now, for those of you with a modern space that's itching for a bit of history, here's the game plan.

Give her the spotlight. Give your antique piece a place of honor. Maybe it's a big old bookcase in the living room or a sideboard in the dining area. This is where making a mood board will come in handy. You may need another piece of furniture to leave the room before bringing something ~~new~~ "old" in.

Give your antique a friend (*cough* the rule of pairs). When you bring in an antique, it should come with a buddy that speaks its language, because keeping it on its own will make the space feel off. Bought a mahogany antique table? Try pairing it with a mahogany side table or an accent bouclé chair with mahogany legs. This way, your antique won't feel like a stranger in your home.

Play with contrast (and juxtapositions!). Shake things up with a bit of contrast. If you're bringing in that mahogany antique table, consider keeping your velvet, modern sculptural chairs for contrast. Or if you are introducing an antique bookcase, place a modern leather or sherpa bench in front of the piece for that new/old contrast.

Keep it cohesive. Your colors and materials should get along. If your antique is dark wood with a warm undertone, make sure you are incorporating woods in your space with the same undertones (whether they are antique or contemporary).

Once you start feeling more comfortable with the principles of pairing and juxtapositions, it will eventually become second nature to you!

BEFORE YOU BUY

Eyeing that antique cabinet or dining table? Before you buy, map out the dimensions with painter's tape at home. This trick gives you a visual sense of how the pieces will fit in your space, so you won't have any regrets after your purchase!

The main feature in this room is undoubtedly the stunning antique mantel, which beautifully contrasts with the contemporary elements throughout the space.

DIRECTOR
JOHN DERIAN
LEONARDO DA VINCI
VERMEER
BRUEGEL
ROBERT MAPPLETHORPE
FORNASETTI
HIRST

BRIGHT IDEAS: YOUR NATURAL LIGHT AND FURNITURE COLORS

Natural light plays a crucial role in determining the colors and types of furniture that will work best in your space. The direction your room faces and the amount of light it receives throughout the day can greatly influence the look and feel of your furniture.

Bright, south-facing rooms. These rooms are bathed in warm, bright light for most of the day. This abundance of natural light allows you to incorporate darker, richer wood tones without the space feeling too heavy. Walnut antique pieces, with their deep, warm hues, can add a touch of elegance and sophistication, complementing the bright ambiance.

Darker, north-facing rooms. North-facing rooms tend to receive cooler, more diffuse light. In these spaces, darker furniture can make the room feel even dimmer and more confined. Opt for lighter wood tones, like oak or maple, to brighten up the space. Lighter furniture can reflect the available light, making the room feel more open and airy.

East-facing rooms. These rooms get bright morning light, which can be quite warm, but the light fades by the afternoon. Choosing furniture in medium wood tones can balance the changing light. Pieces that aren't too dark or too light will maintain their appeal throughout the day.

West-facing rooms. West-facing rooms receive warm, intense light in the late afternoon and evening. To counteract the strong, sometimes harsh light, consider using furniture with cool undertones or lighter finishes to create a balanced look.

Assessing Light Levels. Regardless of direction, the specific amount of light your room gets should influence your choices. Rooms with limited natural light benefit from furniture in lighter shades, which can make the space feel brighter. In contrast, well-lit rooms can handle a mix of light and dark pieces, offering more flexibility in your design.

In this north-facing room with small windows, lighter textures and colors help brighten the space.

THE IMPORTANCE OF FLOOR UNDERTONES

When decorating a space, floor undertones are a *critical* detail that can make all the difference. If something feels "off" in your room, it's often because the undertones don't match. The secret is to align the undertones—whether warm or cool—of your floors with your overall decor.

When you're thrifting for antiques, understanding floor undertones becomes even more important. To determine the undertone of your floors, place a piece of white paper next to them. If the floor appears more yellow or red, it has a warm undertone. If it looks more blue or violet, it's a cool undertone.

With this knowledge, you can choose antiques that complement your floor's undertones. For warm floors, look for pieces with warm finishes, like golden oak or mahogany. These will blend seamlessly and enhance the room's cohesiveness. If your floors have cool undertones, seek out antiques with cooler finishes or materials, like ash or gray-washed wood.

Floor undertones can truly make or break a space. The modern herringbone floor harmonizes elegantly with a vintage cream sofa, tan mantel, cream antique vase, and modern greenish-brown rug.

OLD MEETS BOLD: CONTRAST TEXTURES WITH ANTIQUE FURNITURE

Incorporating a variety of textures is one of my favorite ways to enhance the charm of antique furniture while giving your space a contemporary feel. It's important to never use just one texture in your space—such as all glass or all wood. This can make the room feel flat and monotonous. Instead, mix and match different materials to create a rich, layered look. The interplay of various textures will highlight the unique beauty of each piece!

Here are some ways stunning contrasts can be created with different materials.

Sheepskin. Drape a soft sheepskin throw over an antique wooden chair or bench. The plush texture of the sheepskin creates a luxurious contrast against the solid, hard surface of the wood, adding warmth and comfort.

Bouclé. Use bouclé fabric for modern cushions or an upholstered piece near your antique furniture. The nubby texture of bouclé provides a striking visual and tactile contrast to the smooth, polished surfaces of antiques, adding depth and interest to the space.

Jute. Place a jute rug under a vintage dining table or set of antique chairs. The natural, coarse texture of jute complements the refined details of antique woodwork, bringing a grounded, earthy element to the room.

Glass. Incorporate glass decor pieces like vases, lamps, or coffee tables alongside your antique furniture. The sleek, transparent quality of glass contrasts beautifully with the rich, opaque textures of antique wood and metal, creating a balanced and elegant look.

Stone. Add stone elements, such as a marble-topped side table or stone sculptures, near your antique pieces. The smooth, cool surface of the stone provides a striking contrast to the warm, intricate textures of aged wood and metal.

Metal. Mix in metal accents like silver curtain rods or a metallic floor lamp, picture frames, or lamps. The shiny, reflective surfaces of metals enhance the patina of antique furniture, creating a dynamic interplay between old and new.

This vintage bistro table originally came from an old café in Brooklyn. Vintage stone pieces are always worth the investment. They're timeless and built to last for generations.

Linen partnered with antique or vintage stone is one of my favorite combinations in any home. There's something so romantic about the contrast of textures – different yet both earthy and organic.

REFRESHING YOUR ANTIQUE

Whether it's thrifted, inherited, or just in need of a little love, furniture sometimes needs a good facelift. Refreshing your pieces is a fantastic way to avoid buying new. Here are a few ways to personalize and transform your furniture from drab to fab.

Swap Out or Add New Hardware. Knobs, pulls, handles—these small changes can make a big impact. They're affordable and can modernize your furniture in a snap.

Stain It. If you love your wooden furniture but want a change, consider staining it. Sand it down and choose a new hue. Staining can refresh a piece that feels too dark or outdated. Don't be afraid to explore colorful stains for a unique twist.

Utilize a Furniture Cover. There are so many affordable options for sofas, chairs, and ottomans that can match any decor style and are easy to wash—perfect for homes with kids and pets. I use them with my dog, Seymour, and they're a lifesaver!

Add or Remove Legs. Changing the legs of your furniture can completely alter its vibe. Swap thick, heavy legs for sleek hairpin ones for a modern feel or add legs to a ground-level piece to give it a lift.

Reupholster. Give your upholstered pieces a new lease on life with fresh fabric. Choose modern textiles to transform dated furniture into something contemporary. This can be a DIY project or done professionally for a polished finish.

Cover It Up. Contact paper and peel-and-stick wallpaper are great for adding color and pattern to boring surfaces quickly. These can be especially fun inside shelves and cabinets for a subtle pop. For high-touch surfaces, use these as a last resort since they can bubble and wear over time.

Clean and Polish. Sometimes, all your antique needs is a good cleaning and polish. Use the right cleaners and polishes for the material to restore its original shine (head to **page 156** for more info on care).

Use Furniture Wax. For wooden antiques, a bit of furniture wax can work wonders. It protects and enhances the wood's natural beauty. Apply it sparingly and buff to a lovely sheen.

Protect with Glass Tops. Custom-cut glass tops can protect beautiful antique tables from wear and tear, letting you showcase their original surfaces without worry.

Who says nightstands are the only option beside the bed? An antique desk or dresser can double as a nightstand, offering both functionality and a an old-world touch of contrast in this ultra-modern space.

~~TAKE~~ TECHNIQUE YOUR TIME

You can just take the rule of pairs, juxtapositions, and mismatching and run with those guidelines and be fine. But if you *really* want to nail your redesign, here are some small, yet powerful techniques you could incorporate.

Decorate with a consistent theme. Keep a consistent design theme (when it comes to your contemporary interior), such as minimalism or industrial, to seamlessly integrate antique pieces into the space.

Be mindful of scale and proportion. Ensure that the scale of your modern furniture complements the antique pieces—neither should overpower the other. When in doubt, keep the room's larger items neutral and let the antique piece make the statement. Allow for plenty of negative space around larger antiques to let them stand out and prevent a cluttered look.

Coordinate your colors. Match the color palette of your modern decor with the dominant colors in your antique piece to create a cohesive look. For instance, if the antique has hints of gold, incorporate modern elements with similar gold accents also. Paint walls in neutral tones to create a backdrop that doesn't compete with the intricate details of antique furniture.

Use colors that are next to each other on the color wheel for both antique and modern elements to create a gentle and pleasing contrast. **See page 88** for the color wheel.

Don't let anyone tell you that you can't mix metals. A home should feel lived in, and any lived-in home will have mixed metals. It's all about the rule of pairs and making sure you have an equal amount of both in your space.

Lighten it up. Use bold, contemporary lighting fixtures to draw the eye and create a modern atmosphere around the antique pieces. Combine different types of lighting (ambient, task, and accent) to highlight antique furniture and cast it in a contemporary light.

Update your upholstery. Reupholster antique seating with modern fabrics or patterns to give them a fresh, updated look that still respects the original design.

Contemporary lighting adds a lovely modern touch to this room with antique molding and other original old-home features.

Accessorize smartly.

- Accessorize large antique furniture with modern technology, like a sleek table stand or a minimalist lamp, to bring the piece into the present day.
- Use contemporary rugs to tie the room together, providing a backdrop that complements the antique and modern pieces.
- Place soft, plush modern textiles like throws or pillows on sturdier antique pieces to soften their presence in a modern space.
- Use modern pieces with reflective surfaces near your antiques to brighten the space and add depth.
- Pair large antiques with modern indoor plant arrangements to breathe life into the design and soften the transition between eras.

Work with your wood.

- Repurpose antiques for modern use, such as turning an old sideboard into an entertainment center.
- Match the wood tones of your antiques with modern pieces or contrast light modern woods with dark antique woods for a bold look.
- Commission modern pieces that are designed with nods to the antique's era, creating bespoke harmony between old and new. Or have a carpenter reinterpret a feature from your antique piece into a new furniture item, creating a direct lineage in craftsmanship.

You can never go wrong putting an ultra-modern chair with an antique table.

Group for interest and interaction. Group smaller modern items on or around a large antique piece to create visual interest without clutter. Design the space to be interactive—modern chairs around an antique table invite use and blend function with form.

Essentially, these pieces aren't just furniture; they're characters that bring history, personality, and warmth into your space. The key is to play with balance and contrast, letting each piece shine without overshadowing the rest. Whether you're revamping a family heirloom or introducing a thrifted find into a contemporary setting, the magic happens when you embrace the mix of old and new. So, go ahead—experiment, have fun, and let your space evolve with each unique piece you bring in.

NEW TRICKS FOR OLD PIECES

Accenting with Antiques

SO WE HAVE OUR LARGER ANTIQUE PIECE in our space, and this is my favorite part: accessorizing! Accents are the glue that really makes a space come together. P.S. If you're JUST starting from scratch on your journey of designing with antiques, starting with your accents is a GREAT way to test the waters. Funny enough, this is how I fell in love with designing antiques!

WHAT IS CONSIDERED AN ACCENT ANTIQUE PIECE?

If you are working with any of the below items, you are technically working with an *accent* antique piece. In the interior design business, there are a few pieces of furniture that can be considered either a large furniture piece or an accent to your larger items (think *pianos*).

- **Side tables**
- **Area rugs**
- **Lamps and lighting**
- **Accent or side chairs**
- **Console tables**
- **Hall stands and coatracks**
- **Vanity tables**
- **Chaise lounges and daybeds**
- **Love seats**
- **Fireplaces and mantels**
- **Large trunks and chests**
- **Large framed mirrors**
- **Ornate screens and room dividers**
- **Small secretary desks (under 45 inches)**
- **Grandfather clocks**

LEFT: This antique side table repurposed as a dining table features a glass top and is paired with a mix of modern and traditional chairs for a perfectly balanced feel.
RIGHT: Antique or vintage mirrors are a fantastic alternative to wall art, especially when they reflect art from an opposite wall.

Ok. First, we need to determine if you are 1) accenting a contemporary home WITH large antiques already in the space or 2) accenting a contemporary space with NO large antique furniture.

Let's start with the second. If you are accenting with NO large antique furniture already in place—remember the **rule of pairs**. For example, if you incorporate an antique mahogany side table, make sure to pair it with something else that is antique mahogany in the space. This is the best way to start working those antique accents into your space.

If you're starting from scratch to introduce antiques into your home, I personally think it's easier to start with accents versus large antique pieces. It will help you build confidence as you learn how to pick pieces and naturally incorporate them into your space.

If you already have some large antique furniture, let's break this into five sections.

To reiterate, the combination of metal and wood is simply perfection. If you're starting fresh, an easy formula is pairing antique furniture with modern metal decor or lighting. It's a foolproof way to create a balanced look.

SHUT THE FRONT DOOR

SHUT THE FRONT DOOR
CHOW

WORKING WITH ANTIQUE ACCENT FURNITURE

Whether you are placing antique accents in a space with or without antiques already in it, it's important to consider scale and proportion compared to the items already in the space! Getting this right can transform a room from being disjointed to feeling harmoniously styled.

When integrating smaller antique pieces, like side tables, consoles, or accent chairs, their size in relation to other furnishings in the room is key. For example, you don't want two items the exact same size right next to each other. You will want to vary the heights of your furniture (both accent and large) to help draw the eye up and down in a space!

The concept of visual weight is crucial too. Antique pieces often carry a heavier visual weight due to their unique designs and materials. Balancing these with lighter contemporary pieces ensures the space doesn't feel overwhelmed by any one style. For example, a robust antique wooden chest might be balanced with a sleek modern sofa, creating a visual and stylistic equilibrium.

Lastly, consider the overall function and flow of the room. An antique writing desk needs to not only fit the space physically but also suit the room's usage. Try to pair that antique desk with a modern chair with the same wood undertone.

Wondering what to do with grannie's old dishware? Rather than stashing it away in a cupboard, display it on your shelves alongside some leaning artwork for a charming and personal touch.

YOU'RE ABOUT TO BE FLOORED: DESIGNING WITH ANTIQUE AREA RUGS

Decorating with antique area rugs in a contemporary space is *such* a clever way to add in that "antique" feel without doing much at all. These timeless pieces have the unique ability to literally ground a room while adding a layer of depth and interest that newer rugs might not provide.

First, you need to select the right rug. Look for hues that already complement your existing decor to create a cohesive look. An antique rug doesn't need to match everything in the room perfectly, but it should harmonize with the overall color scheme and undertones in the space. Think about complementary colors.

There are three types of colors: primary, secondary, and tertiary. Primary colors are red, blue, and yellow. They're pure hues that can't be mixed from other colors. The secondary colors orange, green, and violet are made by mixing two primary colors. Tertiary colors are created when a secondary color is mixed with a primary color.

Complementary colors are opposite each other on the color wheel, while analogous colors are next to each other. Use this guide when pairing colors—you can't go wrong with complementary or analogous combinations!

PRO TIP

This might be controversial, but I would only decorate with an antique rug if MOST of the objects on top of it are contemporary. A rule of thumb is to keep all of the large pieces of furniture on top of the rug contemporary, and then you can incorporate antiques with the rug and smaller accent furniture.

This is a great example of how undertones can modernize a heavily antique space. The cool undertones in the fabric and walls bring a vibrant, fresh energy to the room. You can make an even bolder statement in your space by showcasing the same wallpaper behind tall shelves.

Additionally, the size of the rug is crucial in defining spaces within your home. In a living room, for instance, an antique rug can anchor a seating area, creating a cozy, intimate setting. In a studio apartment, it can help define certain areas. Ensure the rug is proportionate to your furniture arrangement; a too-small rug can make the space feel disjointed, while a rug that's adequately sized will unify the room. Basically, size DOES matter.

A good rule of thumb is to have each large piece of furniture touch the rug, typically extending past the first two legs. Ideally, aim for six to twelve inches of rug visible on all sides.

For example, if you have an antique rug, make sure it's large enough so your contemporary sofa's front legs rest on it, with some rug showing around the edges.

You can also consider layering your antique rug over a larger, more neutral carpet for added texture and visual interest. This technique not only protects your antique piece, but also enhances its appearance, making it a focal point. Layering rugs adds depth to your space and can be particularly effective in rooms with a minimalist color scheme, where the texture and patterns of the rug can take center stage!

PRO TIP

Caring for your antique rugs is VITAL. Place them away from direct sunlight to prevent fading and consider professional cleaning to preserve their colors and fibers. With proper care, an antique rug can be a cherished part of your home for generations.

The vintage hutch pairs beautifully with the modern table and chairs in this dining room.

DESIGNING WITH ANTIQUE LIGHTING

BEFORE YOU BUY

While antique lighting adds a visual interest to your space, make sure it meets current lighting standards and efficiency. You may need to rewire vintage fixtures or replace old bulbs with LED options that mimic the warmth of traditional incandescent bulbs. These updates can help preserve the integrity of the antique while making it functional and safe for everyday use. This is where I would consult an electrician.

Now I'm going to contradict myself a bit. In my book, *Shut the Front Door*, I said I don't recommend mixing contemporary and antique lighting in a room. In the spaces I've worked with, it just simplifies things to go one way or the other by letting you nail that specific vibe you're after. Modern lighting (or even vintage) offers up the latest in high-tech and efficiency, and is perfect for a fuss-free, clean look that matches the airy feel of contemporary rooms. On the flip side, going all-in with antique pieces can dial up the charm and bring out that antique character you really want.

Think about where antique lighting will be most effective and aesthetically pleasing in your space. A grand chandelier might make a statement in the entrance hall or dining area, casting a warm, inviting glow, while a pair of antique sconces could add symmetry and sophistication to a living room or bedroom. Old-fashioned table lamps work beautifully on side tables or desks, offering a softer, more localized light source that enhances the ambiance of a room.

If you have a nonworking fireplace, you can make it look more realistic by painting a board matte black and placing it behind the mantel. This simple trick adds depth, creating the illusion of an open space.

With so many lighting options out there, it's easy to feel overwhelmed. But don't worry—I've got you covered.

Ambient. This type of lighting fills the room with light. It's the base layer that makes everything visible. Think chandeliers, pendant lights, table lamps, floor lamps, and recessed lighting.

Task. Just like it sounds, task lighting helps you focus on specific activities. It's more focused and directional. Examples include under-cabinet lights, vanity lights, some sconces, and desk lamps.

Accent. This is my favorite! Accent lighting is all about adding character and highlighting features. Use it to draw attention to artwork, architectural details, or even the light fixture itself. Think wall-mounted art lights, recessed spotlights, LED strips, and decorative sconces.

POINT OF VIEW

When it comes to mixing antiques with modern elements, here is my rule of thumb. I know this is controversial, but this is what has worked best in my designs! If you already have more than one large antique piece in your room, stick to contemporary lighting. If you only have large contemporary pieces in your space, with just a few antique accents, go for all antique lighting if you want!

The "unexpected red theory" is a game-changer for any room that feels like it's missing *something* unique. This bold red modern chandelier coupled with original molding makes a statement all on its own.

LET THERE BE LIGHT: DESIGNING WITH ANTIQUE MIRRORS

Mirrors make any space feel brighter, larger, and more elegant. I have such a girl-crush on mirrors.

Many antique mirrors carry a sense of history and craftsmanship that is hard to find in modern pieces. But consider their placement carefully. The style, material, color, and size of the mirror's frame should complement the overall theme of your space while standing out as a piece of art in its own right.

When it comes to placing an antique mirror in your contemporary space, location is key for maximizing its impact. Ideally, it should be positioned where it can either reflect a view of furniture at most angles, or amplify natural light, such as opposite or near a window. This not only brightens the room but also creates a visual expansion of the space.

There's no hard and fast rule that a mirror must be placed next to something contemporary or antique. The beauty of incorporating such a timeless piece lies in its versatility; it can serve as a stunning contrast against modern decor, or it can complement an existing collection of antique pieces, reinforcing the historical theme. The decision should really be guided by the overall balance you want in your room. Do you want it to stand out as a focal point or to blend in seamlessly?

Layered mirrors. There is no limit to the quantity or room. They're such a unique and playful statement feature that can transform any room. Layer antique or modern together; don't mix styles.

This kitchen has a classy combination of vintage and modern elements. The antique mirror, large vintage cabinet, and vintage crates underneath create a wonderfully playful contrast with the modern granite and tile surfaces.

PICTURE THIS: DESIGNING WITH ANTIQUE ART

Oh, the way people HATE on my antique art on social media! But I am SUCH an antique portrait girly. I think part of my heart feels that if someone's portrait can't be with its rightful descendants, I can give it a good home somewhere else. Regardless, I know antique portraits are not for everyone, even though they do bring such character, and stories (real or imagined) into your home.

There are other types of antique art you can incorporate into your space, however. Landscapes offer tranquility and a sense of openness. Still lifes and genre art can introduce classical elegance and dynamic stories, further enriching your decor.

Consider mixing up your display methods—layering pieces on walls, mixing frame styles for added interest, or even going frameless to let the art's authenticity shine. For a bold statement, art on the ceiling transforms the space, merging past and present in a uniquely personal way. By carefully selecting and placing these various types of antique art, you'll weave a rich narrative that enhances the aesthetic of your home.

Frames don't always have to be level. Intentionally angling or leaning art can add a fun and dynamic touch.

A BALANCING ACT: GETTING CONTEMPORARY TO PLAY WELL WITH ANTIQUE ACCENT PIECES

Below are a few of my favorite ways to use both contemporary and antique accent pieces in a home.

Mix contemporary art with antique frames. Use modern art within an antique frame or place contemporary sculptures atop an antique table to fuse different eras.

Contrast your lighting. Illuminate antiques with modern lighting fixtures, like track lights or pendant lamps, to bring a contemporary edge to the space.

Add modern accents. Decorate antique tables with modern accessories, such as geometric vases or minimalist candle holders.

Use rugs as a unifier. Have large antique furniture? Use contemporary rugs to tie the room together, providing a backdrop that complements the antique and modern pieces.

Think of functional conversions. Repurpose antiques for modern use, such as turning an old sideboard into an entertainment center.

Create a period contrast. Place a piece from a different but specific modern design period, like mid-century modern, with your antique to create a conversation between the two periods.

Do you have a modern kitchen with modern kitchenware? Add contrast by displaying your modern glassware on an antique shelf – it's a delicious blend of old and new.

Consider shared historical elements. Integrate modern pieces that have a historical reference or a silhouette that echoes the antique's era, bridging the gap between old and new.

Playfully pair your accessories. Don't be afraid to balance whimsical modern art or accessories with serious antique pieces to add a touch of levity.

Integrate your architecture. Commingle the antique piece with modern architectural elements like built-in shelves or contemporary wall treatments.

Drape dramatically. Use modern drapery to frame an antique window seat or chair, providing a fresh backdrop that highlights the piece.

Form artistic links. Select modern art pieces that mimic the artistry or subject matter of the antique, forging a visual and thematic connection.

Antiquing your space with accent pieces is all about striking the right balance and having fun with it. Whether you're starting small or already have some statement pieces, these accents bring personality, charm, and history into any room. Let your creativity lead the way—mix and match, play with scale, and embrace the unexpected. Remember, it's not just about filling a room but telling a story that's uniquely yours.

Candlesticks, candlesticks, candlesticks! They're the ultimate way to add a romantic touch to any tabletop or mantel. The plentiful electric options available eliminate both the fire hazard and drippings inherent with wax candles.

LE ROMAN
DE
TRISTAN
LES ROMANS

SHOW AND TELL

The Art of Display

SO WE HAVE LARGE FURNITURE, accent pieces, but what about decorative objects? Things like dishware, glassware, decorative boxes, vases, collections, etc.?

Decorating with decorative objects is probably my favorite part of designing a space. I'd like to think of these objects as the varnish to your painting: It's what pulls everything together!

PRO TIP

Only have a few antique accents? Grouping smaller antiques together can create a sense of intentionality in their display. Rather than scattering single items throughout a space, consider dedicating a section or piece of furniture to showcase a collection of antiques. This approach not only highlights your treasured finds but also adds a cohesive element to the decor.

A Nod to Nancy

You know when you're watching a Nancy Myers film and you can't help but fall for the spaces just as much as the characters? They've got that lived-in vibe that feels like a warm hug (P.S. *The Holiday* is one of my favorite films!). Her scenes aren't just a set; they tell stories with shelves that look like they've been filled over Sunday mornings at impromptu flea market hauls, and with items passed down from family members—not just one quick spree at the Home Goods store. It's that authentic, cozy feel we all crave.

Don't forget to think beyond your walls. Doors and ceilings are amazing surfaces to display art and add an unexpected touch to your space!

THE TRICK OF LAYERING

Layering is an amazing way to blend contemporary style with antique pieces, creating a rich and dynamic look. If you're new to designing with antiques, layering is a great way to practice and get used to incorporating both! Here are a few tips to master the art of layering.

Rugs. Layering an antique rug over a larger modern one can create a stunning focal point. The contrast between the intricate patterns of the antique rug and the simplicity of the modern one adds depth and interest to your floor space.

Books and Decor. Use antique books as stylish bases for modern decor items. Stack a few vintage books and place a sleek, contemporary vase or sculpture on top. This combination showcases the charm of the past while keeping the look fresh and current.

Artwork. Mix and match frames and artwork styles. Hang a contemporary piece of art next to an ornate antique frame. The juxtaposition of styles can create a visually appealing gallery wall that tells a unique story. (PSST—you can also layer your frames on top of each other by using different-sized nails!)

Furniture. Pair modern furniture with antique accents. For example, drape a contemporary throw over a classic armchair or place a modern lamp on a vintage side table. This blending of styles keeps the space feeling balanced and cohesive.

Layered artwork is hands-down my favorite statement to incorporate into any space I design!

DISHING OUT

Let's talk about dishware and chinaware—it's not just for Thanksgiving anymore. Imagine your grandma's floral plates, or those quirky mugs you picked up on vacation, out in the open, telling the tale of how you found those items. You can pop them on a wall rack or let them peek out of an open cupboard.

You can place your favorite plates on a book display as if they were literary works or arrange them on open shelving next to a stack of worn cookbooks.

Also, did you know you can hang plates as artwork? Plate hangers are very inexpensive and can be found online or in almost any craft store.

Or simply use a plate rack to display your most cherished dishware.

There are so many amazing ways to take your beautiful antique dishes out of the closed cupboard and use them as decorative objects.

Varying heights and shapes of objects displayed on shelves adds interest. Layering items in front of and behind each other adds depth and creates a cozy, lived-in vibe.

BOX IT UP

Now, about those decorative boxes and vases. They're the silent narrators of your space. That little jade box from the antique shop down the street or the hand-painted vase from your trip abroad—they're not just "stuff." They're snippets of your life's script. Don't just line them up like soldiers on a shelf. Mix them in with other items, maybe a stack of vintage postcards or a modern sculpture, letting each piece stand out without the clutter.

Also, vases aren't just for tables. You can display a collection of vases on the floor with some faux florals inside.

And those decorative boxes? Whether they're on your coffee table, displayed on a side table, or layered on top of some books on a shelf, these items are just as functional as they are decorative. (In fact, there's not one box in my own home without something inside of it!)

Vintage purses aren't meant to be tucked away in your closet. Show them off on your walls or shelves.

VERSACE
LIGHT YEARS

BOOK ~~NERDS~~ NOOKS

Books—they're not just meant for your bookshelves. Stacked, leaned, or color-coded, I like to think of them as bricks and mortar! For example, stack some books under a table lamp on your nightstand or a decorative object on your coffee table. A stack of books on a chair under some florals? Absolutely. Leaned on the floor up against a wall? Perfect. Books are the secret decorators of your space.

Have you ever seen a Nancy Meyers' home without books? I didn't think so!

Need to hide clutter under an open cabinet or shelf? Vintage curtains are a charming and practical solution.

CANDLESTICKS AND CURIOS

Finally, those candlesticks, decorative objects, and all the quirky little things you've got scattered about. They might seem random, but together, they're the finishing touches. Cluster them on an end table or let a candlestick collection march down the runner of a dining table. Display items on your coffee table or on top of a console. Or better yet, place them on a shelf—which is what we will talk about next!

Small mementos, like magnifying glasses, decorative boxes, or opera glasses, can double as unique and meaningful decor.

RIGHT: Books on a shelf don't always have to be closed. Why not open a few to pages with interesting art or photos to add a personal touch to your shelf or table? OPPOSITE: When going all-in with an antique look for shelves, aim to make them feel lived in, for a truly organic vibe.

TAKING A SHELFIE

When it comes to shelving, there's a secret: layering. On a shelving unit or étagère, if everything's on the same plane, things get boring fast. And keeping items on the same plane is usually what most people instinctively do. But instead, layer it up. Put some objects in front, some behind. Let a small painting lean against a stack of books or set a vase in front of a framed piece of art, and suddenly, you've got depth. It's all about making a space feel collected, layered over time, not curated in a single afternoon.

In the end, it's all about creating a space that's a mirror of your character. So have some fun with it!

Flour.

MEMENTOS MATTER

This was my favorite section to write, but also the most challenging. As you may know, I return lost heirlooms to families. Well, mostly "mementos" to families. I'll find things like letters, photographs, diaries, and jewelry and track the living descendants to return these items that once belonged to their ancestor.

Many people keep such cherished items hidden away in a shoebox under the bed or in a drawer they open, at most, once a year. If you want to incorporate these treasures into your design, there's *always* a way.

LEFT: Clothes don't have to stay in the closet! Show off your favorite dress or outfit on a beautiful hanger and display it like a piece of art. RIGHT: Exhibit a vintage oversized book on a modern easel to create a unique statement in your room.

Displaying Photographs

Photographs are probably the most common type of memento, and they offer endless possibilities for creative display. Here are a few ideas on how to incorporate them, aside from the generic gallery wall.

I have a meaningful keepsake and home goods line, and one product I offer is "This is Not a Coffee Table Book" – a cleverly designed coffee-table book that's actually a customizable photo album inside. But you can DIY something similar. A simple three-ring binder can do the trick. Or, for something with more charm, try thrifting an older vintage or antique photo album. Older pieces often have with lovely details that add a unique touch.

Create unique photo albums. If your photos are small enough, consider displaying them in a photo-album-meets-coffee-table book. Your guests will be pleasantly surprised when they open a book and see instead your cherished memories or mementos!

Display a sketch board. This idea came to me when I was thrifting last summer. I saw a vintage sketch clipboard and immediately thought how cool it would be to display a large non-framed photograph or piece of art.

Design a large pinboard. I LOVE a good pinboard—and it's something I don't think can ever go out of style. Consider pinning a mix of your favorite photographs, and other little mementos like ticket stubs and dried florals on a pinboard. This is a great way to tell a full story using many different objects!

Showcasing Jewelry

Layer jewelry over a vase. This hack of mine went viral on Pinterest years ago! And for good reason. Instead of storing your jewelry in a drawer or box, display your necklaces over a vase. This functional idea instantly upgrades a plain surface and creates an immediate feature statement. (This same idea can work with antique or vintage busts also.)

Display on a tray. Another idea is to use decorative trays or bowls to display jewelry on dressers or side tables. This not only keeps them within easy reach but also turns them into part of your decor. Choose containers that complement your overall design aesthetic—vintage glass bowls for a classic look, or sleek metallic trays for a modern touch.

Avoid leaving jewelry by a window, as prolonged exposure to sun can cause metals to tarnish and gemstones to fade over time. Additionally, fluctuating temperatures and humidity near windows can accelerate damage.

Preserving and Displaying Letters

Frame them. Letters and handwritten notes carry a deeply personal touch, and there are several creative ways to incorporate them into your decor. Consider framing a particularly meaningful letter or a series of postcards and displaying them on a wall or mantel.

Place them in a bowl. This might sound strange but hear me out. For letters that aren't too fragile (this could be non-family heirlooms or just love letters you like to collect), you can place them in a large bowl on your coffee table. This is such a great conversation starter.

POINT OF VIEW

Letters are my favorite items to return to families. Someone's first-hand accounts can tell you things about a person that no record could ever tell you.

For fragile letters, consider using UV-protective glass to preserve them while framing. If they're *really* delicate, display a high-quality copy and store the original in a protective sleeve to prevent further deterioration.

Curating Collections

Collections of items—whether they are seashells from your travels, vintage postcards, or a bowl of matchbooks—add such a unique character to your home. These little items, which some may think are too small to make a difference, are really what make your home yours and not a copy of someone else's.

Maybe you have a collection of matchbooks. I love the idea of displaying them in a bowl, but you can also place little magnets on the back and place them on a magnetic surface like your fridge.

As for postcards, you can display them in a photo album instead of leaving them inside a drawer collecting dust. If you want to get a bit crazy, you can line the inside of an open vintage suitcase with postcards, propping it open for a nostalgic and portable display.

Decorating and designing with mementos and memorabilia is more than just an aesthetic choice; it's about creating a home that reflects your unique journey and the people who have shaped it. Again, these mementos and keepsakes are what make your home **yours and not a copy of someone else's**. No one else can have those letters from your great-grandmother or those photographs your grandfather passed down to you. Embrace your mementos and celebrate them in your home!

Organize vintage books by color to create an eye-catching display on your shelves.

INSIDE NORTH KOREA
SO FAR SO GOUDE
CIVILIZATION

The Grapes of Wrath
COME INTO MY PARLOR
THE STREETS OF OLD NEW YORK
DEATH OF A SALESMAN
ORPHEUS
MYTHS OF THE WORLD
QUO VADIS?
Lust for Life
Kara Walker: My Complement, My Enemy, My Oppressor, My Love
FREDERIC MORTON
DIANE ARBUS
TO BROOKLYN WITH LOVE
GERALD GREEN
TO KILL A Mockingbird
HARPER LEE

LEONARDO DA VINCI
VERMEER
KING'S VIEWS OF NEW YORK 1896–1915 & BROOKLYN 1905
Les châteaux de l'Île-de-France
INTERIEURS ANCIENS ET RUSTIQUES
Gauguin
MOZART—SONATAS
BRUEGEL
ROBERT MAPPLETHORPE
Georges Bloch
Pablo Picasso
Catalogue de l'œuvre gravé et lithographié 1904–1967

JEAN PROUVÉ
JEAN PROUVÉ

ALL THAT GLITTERS IS OLD

Sourcing Your Antiques

NAVIGATING THE VIBRANT CHAOS of flea markets, auctions, and the boundless expanse of online marketplaces might seem like hunting for needles in haystacks but have no fear! This chapter is your secret map to uncovering treasures with stories as rich as any passed-down heirloom.

But before we get into "where" to get these items, we need to learn how to value and assess items.

VALUING ANTIQUES AND VINTAGE ITEMS

The valuation of antiques is a complex process that intertwines historical significance, rarity, age, condition, and provenance. Contrary to popular belief, an item's age is just one of many factors in determining its value. Collectors and appraisers (if we're going that far!) also consider the story behind the piece.

Rarity adds value, as does demand, and an item that is both rare and sought after in the current market will command a higher price. Condition plays a critical role, too; items in pristine condition or with an appropriate patina that reflects gentle use are typically valued higher than those with damage or excessive wear. Let's get into the details.

PRO TIP

The Google Image Search function is fantastic when on the hunt for antique pieces. Either download the photo of the item you want (if you are purchasing it online) or take a photo of it yourself and upload it to Google Image Search.

Within seconds, similar photos of potentially the exact same item will pop up. You can see others who have listed this item for sale, what they are pricing it at, or furniture enthusiasts who have written a description and history of that exact piece.

Placing large artwork on the floor and leaning it against the wall is a great way to draw the eye to different levels and add depth to your space.

How to Identify Furniture Age

Determining the age of a piece is good to know when dealing with antiques. Different time periods were marked by different craftsmanship techniques, and identifying the age of a piece can also lead to a deeper appreciation of the artistry.

Although it's always best to have an expert verify a piece's age, here are some signs when trying to put a time period on an antique.

Joinery and Construction Techniques

Whenever I am trying to identify the age of a piece, especially wood, I always start with how the drawers are constructed. And this might be the only thing you need to do!

DOVETAIL JOINTS

Dovetail joints were commonly used in drawers from the seventeenth century onward. The size and spacing of dovetails can provide clues to the age of a piece of furniture, but not all dovetails are created equal.

Hand-cut dovetails (Pre-1860s). Prior to the mid-nineteenth century, dovetails were typically hand-cut. These dovetails exhibit irregularity in their spacing and shape, reflecting the craftsmanship of the woodworker. They may not be perfectly symmetrical, and the cuts may show slight variations.

Machine-cut dovetails (Late-nineteenth century onward). With the advent of machinery and industrialization, machine-cut dovetails became more common. These dovetails are typically uniform in size and shape, as machines produce precise, consistent cuts. These will look almost flawless when you look at them!

Above are two examples of handmade / hand-cut dovetail joints.

SCREWS

Just the presence of screws instead of handmade nails can indicate a piece from the nineteenth century or later.

GLUE BLOCKS AND BRACKETS

The use of glue blocks and brackets to reinforce joints became more common in the nineteenth century.

Upholstery and Fabric

Identifying the age of upholstered and fabric furniture can be challenging, but there are several key factors and techniques you can use to get a sense of when a piece might have been made. In full honesty, I always get an expert opinion on fabric but it's worth noting the different eras and common styles here.

FABRIC PATTERNS AND STYLES

Victorian era (1837–1901). Look for elaborate, ornate patterns and heavy, rich fabrics like brocade and velvet. Dark colors such as deep reds, purples, and greens were popular during this period.

Art deco (1920s–1930s). Art deco furniture often features bold, geometric patterns and luxurious materials like silk and satin. Colors tend to be vibrant and include metallic accents.

Mid-century modern (1940s–1960s). Mid-century modern upholstery is characterized by clean lines, simple geometric patterns, and solid, earthy colors. Fabrics like tweed and wool were common.

1970s–1980s. These decades saw the rise of bold, colorful patterns, often in synthetic materials like polyester. Floral prints, large plaids, and bright hues were popular.

Contemporary (1990s–present). Contemporary upholstery often features neutral colors, sleek designs, and a wide range of fabric choices, including microfiber, leather, and synthetic blends.

UPHOLSTERY TECHNIQUES

Hand-tied springs or coiled springs are often indicative of older furniture (pre-twentieth century). Modern furniture may use zigzag or sinuous springs.

Plywood and particleboard are materials commonly used in modern upholstery, whereas older pieces might have solid wood frames.

Look for signs of craftsmanship. Hand-stitching and hand-tufting were common in older furniture, while newer pieces may rely on machine stitching and construction.

UPHOLSTERY MATERIALS

Determine the type of padding used. Horsehair and cotton were commonly used in antique furniture, while foam and synthetic materials are typical in modern pieces.

Check the underside of the upholstery for a label or manufacturer's mark, which can provide valuable information about the piece's age. Google to the rescue!

Patina and Wear

Patina refers to the surface sheen and texture that develops on the exterior of an object over time. It's a combination of wear, oxidation, and natural aging processes that give an item a distinct, often desirable, appearance.

NATURAL AGING

As wood, metal, or other materials are exposed to the environment and human touch, they undergo subtle changes. For example, wood might develop a warm, aged glow, and metals can acquire a soft, tarnished luster. Wood also tends to lose its shine over time. So, if you come across a piece that looks antique, but you can practically see your own reflection in it, it's probably more modern. A great example is the davenport reproduction from the 1950s. A davenport is a tiny writing desk used by Victorian women and was popular during the eighteenth century.

COLOR CHANGES

Patina can result in color changes, such as darkening or mellowing of wood, brass, or copper. These shifts in color can be subtle but are distinctive to each material.

TEXTURE

Patina often involves the development of a unique texture. Wood might become smoother with age, while metals may show signs of fine pitting or wear.

Imagine you have a wooden dining table passed down through generations. The table's top surface exhibits a warm, slightly worn appearance, with subtle scratches and fine cracks in the wood. The legs also show signs of wear near the floor, where people's feet have brushed against them over the years. This consistent, natural aging indicates that the table is a genuine antique with authentic patina and wear (and as a bonus, providing a connection to its history and previous owners).

WEAR

Wear, as you've probably guessed, is the physical effects of use on the surface of an object. It includes scratches, scuffs, dents, and other marks that occur over time.

NATURAL PATTERNS

The wear on a piece of furniture can follow natural patterns, such as the arms of a chair showing more wear than the backrest or the edges of a table exhibiting signs of use.

CONSISTENCY

Genuine wear tends to be consistent with the piece's function and purpose. For example, a writing desk might have ink stains or impressions from pen nibs. Authentic patina and wear tend to be uniform across the entire piece. Reproductions or newer items might lack this consistent aging, although replicas may try to mimic this.

Keep in mind that some antique furniture may have undergone restoration, which can include refinishing and repairs. These areas may appear different from the rest of the piece.

PRO TIP

The overall wear and patina of a piece can easily reveal its age. Older pieces may have developed a natural patina, while more recent pieces may lack this aged look.

PRO TIP

If you find that the wood used in hidden areas of furniture pieces, like the undersides, matches the primary wood used throughout the piece, there's a higher likelihood that it's a reproduction!

WHITE & RED OAK
CHERRY
ASH
MAPLE
BIRCH
TEAK
WALNUT
PINE
CEDAR

Wood Types

Genuine antique furniture typically features a practice where different types of wood were used strategically. Back in the day, using valuable wood for concealed parts of a piece didn't make economic sense. To assess the authenticity of a piece, inspect the undersides of chairs and the interiors of drawers for variations in wood types.

In addition, woodwork done by hand is easy to spot in carved, wood details. Asymmetry is a **good thing** when it comes to wood!

Even the type of wood can be an indicator of a piece's age. Different woods were favored during different periods. I'm not going to lie, I have never used wood as a determining factor for an age of a piece besides items made from cherry and maple. This is something the experts are fluent in. But, for the purpose of this book, I think it's important to include, as it's historically fun to know!

Oak (medieval to early eighteenth century). Oak was the dominant wood in early English and American furniture.

Walnut (late seventeenth to early eighteenth century). Walnut gained popularity during the late seventeenth century, known as the William and Mary period.

Mahogany (eighteenth century). The Georgian and Chippendale periods saw a surge in the use of mahogany.

Cherry and Maple (early nineteenth century). These woods were common during the Federal and Empire periods.

Again, when in doubt, consult an expert appraiser or antique dealer. They have the knowledge to quickly help pinpoint the age of your furniture accurately!

EASY WAYS TO SPOT A POOR-QUALITY PIECE OF FURNITURE

Spotting poor-quality furniture can save you from investing in pieces that won't stand the test of time. Here are some easy ways to identify a low-quality piece of furniture.

Flimsy Construction. Check the joints and connections. Poor-quality furniture often features weak or wobbly joints, such as staples, nails, or glue instead of sturdy techniques like dovetail or mortise-and-tenon joints. (However, if you're looking for handmade or antique pieces, be wary of perfect dowels and dovetails, as this indicates a machine-made piece. It doesn't necessarily mean it's bad quality—it just might not be what you're actually looking for.)

Lightweight. Pick up the piece. Lightweight furniture is often made from inferior materials like particleboard or MDF (medium-density fiberboard). Genuine wood furniture tends to be heavier.

Lack of Solid Wood. Examine the edges and corners. If you see veneer peeling away or particleboard exposed, it's a sign of lower-quality construction.

Weak Back Panels. Inspect the back of the piece. Low-quality furniture may have thin or poorly fitted back panels that can affect stability.

Unfinished or Rough Interiors. Open drawers and cabinets to see if the interiors are finished and smooth. Quality pieces have finished interiors, while poor-quality ones may be rough or unfinished inside.

Lack of Detail. Examine the details and finishing. Low-quality pieces often lack intricate details, moldings, or well-applied finishes.

Plywood Backing. Check the backing of cabinets or bookshelves. Plywood backing can indicate lower quality compared to solid wood.

The intricate desk versus the simple drawers highlights the difference in craftsmanship between the two pieces.

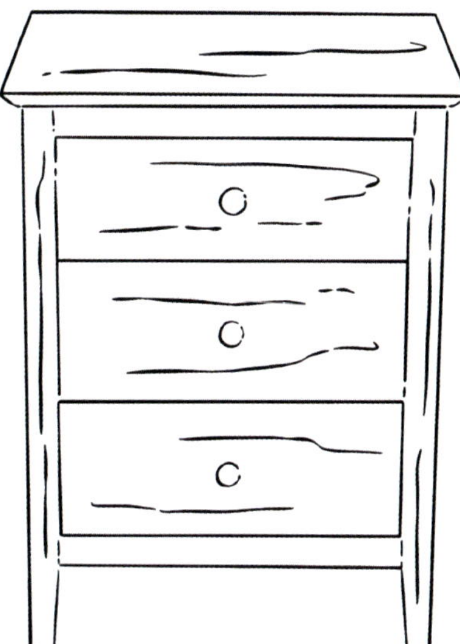

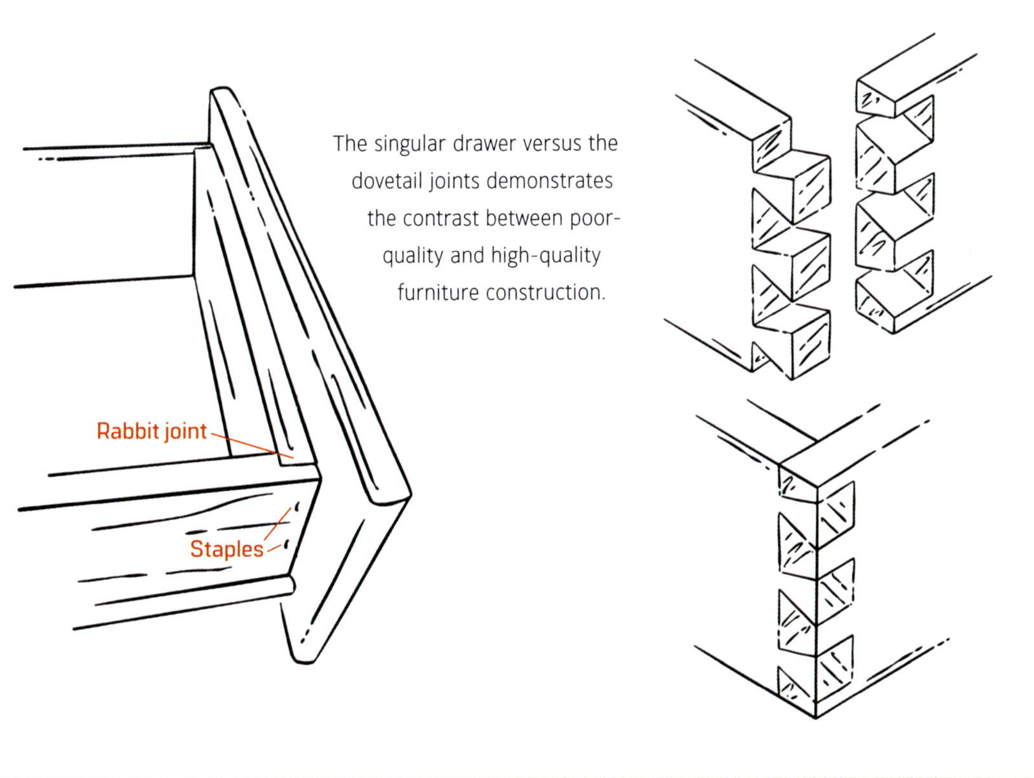

The singular drawer versus the dovetail joints demonstrates the contrast between poor-quality and high-quality furniture construction.

WHERE TO SHOP

When shopping for antiques, be cautious of the elaborate backstories that sometimes come with a piece—especially if there's no paper trail to support it. Sellers might weave a tale to boost the appeal, but don't let that be the deciding factor. Remember, you don't need a perfectly crafted history to fall in love with an antique. Often, part of the fun is imagining the life it led before it found its way to you, or even creating your own story for it. Your personal connection is what truly matters.

Online

Online resale and auction marketplaces like Facebook Marketplace, Craigslist, Mercari, Depop, Chairish, 1stDibs, eBay, LiveAuctioneers, and Invaluable, let you offer and bid on a wide array of items, often landing deals at lower prices. These sites have completely revolutionized the antique-hunting game. I mean, what's better than finding your dream antique dresser while sitting in your pajamas in the comfort of your own living space? (And I might or might not be in my pajamas as I'm writing this.)

PRO TIP

On Facebook Marketplace, the terms "vintage" and "antique" are used interchangeably by many sellers and buyers.

Moreover, for those who find the competitive world of actual flea markets daunting, digital marketplaces (like on Facebook) offer a gentler introduction to bidding. The process is transparent, less pressured, and offers the chance to participate without the fast-paced, high-stakes environment of live auctions. It's a fantastic way to build your confidence in making bids and negotiations.

PRO TIP

Auction-snipe software can be a game-changer for online bidding. It will automatically place a last-second bid for you within your budget to increase your chances of winning. Gixen and Auction Sniper are my two favorites!

But the best part of online shopping for antiques? The item doesn't need to be near you! If a must-have find is too far away—services like uShip can pick up and deliver if the seller doesn't ship themselves. Just list your price on the website, and shippers will bid if it suits their route and budget. I've even shipped big items coast-to-coast for just $200!

BACKSTORY

On an auction site, this dresser was listed $3,000, but I was able to negotiate it down to $1,500.

In person

Now, let's get into the in-person shopping. Flea markets, antique stores, and estate sales are going to be your main objectives.

Flea Markets

Flea markets are hot spots for secondhand goods like decor, books, and art. Do you go to the same ones often? Befriend the vendors for potential deals! To locate nearby markets, check out fleamarket.com.

Negotiating at flea markets can be daunting at first, but it becomes easier with practice and by building relationships with sellers. Here's a streamlined approach.

- Always be polite but start with an offer lower than your budget to allow room for negotiation.
- Present your offer with cash in hand; it's more tempting for the seller to accept.
- Keep your excitement under wraps. Showing too much interest might weaken your bargaining position.
- My favorite tip: If the price isn't right, begin to walk away. Often sellers will lower the price to make the sale.

And it doesn't just stop at flea markets: antique stores/ malls are curated havens for timeless treasures, each piece with its own backstory.

PRO TIP

One thrifting mantra to buy only items you'll love and use is the One Dollar Rule. At a flea market, if you hesitate on a fifteen-dollar find, ask yourself, "Will I use this fifteen times?" If yes, feel great about getting it! If you can honestly say no, let it go.

PRO TIP

If negotiating isn't your strong suit, a little prep can go a long way. Scope out the going rates for items like yours. Reach out to the seller with a genuine message—being relatable can make a difference. Then, present a fair offer, a bit below your budget to leave room for negotiation. Keep it realistic to show you're serious.

Antique Stores and Malls

Usually these are large establishments that offer a collective space for multiple vendors to sell antiques and collectibles. They operate similarly to traditional malls, but instead of contemporary retail stores, they house a variety of booths or stalls, each run by a different vendor specializing in vintage goods.

Here's how they typically work:

Vendor booths. Vendors rent out spaces or booths in the mall to display and sell their items. These spaces are like mini-shops within the larger mall, each with a unique selection of merchandise.

Absentee vendors. Often the individual vendors are not physically present at their booths. They set up their displays and price their items, but the day-to-day sales are handled by the mall's staff.

Diverse inventory. Since each vendor curates their own selection, shoppers can find a wide assortment of antiques and vintage items, ranging from furniture and artwork to jewelry and home decor.

Centralized checkout. Customers don't pay at each booth. Instead, they bring the items to a centralized checkout area managed by the mall's staff, similar to a consignment shop.

Estate Sales

Meanwhile, estate sales can be goldmines for antiques, offering everything from vintage jewelry to classic furniture, often with the chance to haggle. Estate sales often happen because of the death or relocation of a family member who was living alone, but also occur because of people moving abroad or across country or simply downsizing.

Estate sales are where you can buy items directly from a home, often at lower prices since you're bypassing the middleman (like a vintage reseller or a vendor at the flea market). Websites like www.estatesales.net are invaluable for locating sales, offering filters by location and date, plus preview photos to gauge if it's worth attending. Some also host online auctions, but watch for local pickup terms. Some sellers might also choose to conduct an auction-type estate sale.

Estate sales are VERY competitive and are not for the faint of heart! Arrive early to beat dealers and resellers to the prime picks. Plan your transport and budget ahead, as sales typically don't reserve items. Head straight for large furniture upon entry, grabbing the ticket for items you want. Remember, it's first-come, first-served, so don't hesitate to claim tickets for desired pieces.

Other Ways to Obtain Antiques

Another way to obtain those vintage items and antiques, especially from family or friends, is through thoughtful conversations about heirlooms. Encouraging open dialogue with relatives—particularly parents—about how they want their belongings distributed can help avoid misunderstandings. Some may already have preferences or promises in place for certain items, while others might not have considered it yet. These conversations are not just practical but can also offer a meaningful opportunity to learn the stories behind the furniture and heirlooms, making them even more special.

This is why I have a "family heirloom" section in the Time Capsule Journal I sell. This journal allows your loved one to record their entire life story and family history, and there's a section dedicated to pasting in photos of important family heirlooms and writing the importance of that item.

Conversations with family members are especially important because, unfortunately, family drama often arises around who gets what after someone passes. Misunderstandings or unspoken expectations can cause rifts, and in some cases, it can lead to one person gaining access to the estate and selling everything off, leaving the rest of the family with nothing. These situations are heartbreaking, and they're often preventable with the right discussions and legal measures in place.

This is why I highly recommend families consider creating a trust rather than relying solely on a will. A trust offers more protection because it outlines exactly how and when assets will be distributed, keeping things more controlled and less susceptible to manipulation or mismanagement. Unlike a will, which goes through probate, a trust avoids public proceedings and can ensure a smoother transfer of heirlooms and belongings. It's a proactive way to preserve both the estate *and* family harmony.

BACKSTORY

In my years of returning lost heirlooms to families, I've encountered many difficult situations. I've tried to help families navigate the process of reclaiming items from museums that estranged relatives had donated without their consent. I've also worked with a daughter who lost all of her mother's jewelry and artwork to her brother, who took everything from their mother's home after she passed. These experiences highlight just how important it is to have clear conversations and legal safeguards in place to protect cherished family items.

HANDLE WITH CARE

Preserving and Restoring Antiques

TO KEEP YOUR TREASURES LOOKING THEIR BEST, it's essential to understand how to preserve and restore them properly. Whether you're working with wooden furniture, delicate fabrics, stone surfaces, or intricate glass, each material has its own needs. Let's dive into the best ways to care for these cherished items so they can continue to grace your home for years to come.

CARING FOR ANTIQUE WOOD: THE BASICS OF PROTECTION AND RESTORATION

Wooden antiques are classics—think dining tables, cabinets, armoires, and chests. They have stood the test of time but require the right care to maintain their beauty. Sunlight and humidity are wood's biggest enemies. Direct sunlight can cause wood to fade and dry out, while high humidity can lead to warping and cracking. Place wooden pieces away from direct sunlight and maintain a stable environment with consistent humidity levels, ideally between 40 to 60 percent. If you live in a dry climate, consider a room or whole-house humidifier to not only protect your furniture but to maintain a healthier environment for humans too.

When it comes to restoring wood, start by cleaning the surface with a soft, dry cloth to remove dust. For deeper cleaning, use a damp cloth with a mild soap solution, followed by a dry cloth. If the wood is stained or has a worn finish, sanding is a crucial step. Use fine-grit sandpaper and always sand in the direction of the grain to avoid scratches. After sanding, you can apply a stain to enhance the wood's natural color or a clear varnish to protect the surface. Waxing can add a layer of protection and give the wood a beautiful, soft sheen. Apply a thin layer of furniture wax with a cloth, then buff it to a shine.

PRO TIP

If you're dealing with an antique piece with intricate carvings, use a soft-bristled brush to get into the crevices without damaging the details.

FABRIC AND UPHOLSTERY: BRINGING VINTAGE TEXTILES BACK TO LIFE

Antique fabrics and upholstery can add a cozy, nostalgic feel to any room, but they're also prone to wear and tear. Regular maintenance is key. Use a vacuum with a brush attachment to remove dust and dirt from fabric surfaces. For spills or stains, spot cleaning with a mild detergent is usually sufficient. Always test a small, inconspicuous area first to ensure the cleaner won't damage the fabric.

If your upholstered pieces are looking tired or have suffered significant damage, consider reupholstering. Choose fabrics that are both durable and complementary to the era of the piece. For instance, a Victorian chair might look stunning in velvet, while a mid-century piece might call for a more contemporary fabric like linen or leather. Reupholstering not only refreshes the look but can also improve the comfort and lifespan of the piece.

PRO TIP

Use UV-protective window treatments or place antique fabric pieces away from direct sunlight to prevent fading over time.

ART
ART

STONE AND MARBLE: MAINTAINING THAT TIMELESS ELEGANCE

Stone surfaces, like marble tabletops or limestone sculptures, are elegant and timeless but require careful maintenance to stay in pristine condition. Stone is porous, meaning it can easily absorb spills and stains. Always use coasters, place mats, and trivets to protect stone surfaces from moisture and heat. For routine cleaning, use a pH-neutral cleaner and a soft cloth. Avoid using acidic cleaners like vinegar or lemon juice, which can etch the surface and cause dull spots.

If you're dealing with stubborn stains or discoloration, a baking soda poultice can be effective. Mix baking soda with water to create a paste, apply it to the stained area, cover it with plastic wrap, and leave it for 24 to 28 hours. This method draws out the stain without damaging the stone. Regularly sealing stone surfaces is also crucial. A good stone sealant will provide a protective barrier against spills and stains, keeping your surfaces looking fresh.

PRO TIP

For stone pieces in outdoor settings, consider covering them during harsh weather or moving them indoors to prevent erosion and wear.

The deVOL Kitchen

ART AND FRAMES: PROTECTING YOUR MASTERPIECES

Antique artwork and frames require special care to maintain their beauty and value. Always keep art out of direct sunlight to prevent fading. Use UV-protective glass when framing valuable pieces to shield them from harmful rays. Dust frames regularly with a soft, dry cloth, and for the artwork itself, use a soft brush to remove dust gently.

If you notice significant damage, like cracks, flaking paint, or mold, it's best to consult a professional restorer. They have the skills and knowledge to repair these issues without compromising the artwork. When hanging artwork, choose spots away from heat sources like radiators or fireplaces, which can cause warping or cracking.

PRO TIP

Regularly check the backs of framed artwork for signs of moisture damage or pests, which can be common issues in older homes.

METAL ANTIQUES: RESTORING SHINE WITHOUT LOSING CHARACTER

Metal antiques, such as brass candlesticks, copper pots, or iron bed frames, develop a patina over time that adds character. If you prefer a polished look, use a metal polish appropriate for the type of metal. For example, brass and copper can be cleaned with a mixture of lemon juice and baking soda. Apply the mixture with a soft cloth, rinse thoroughly, and buff to a shine. For iron pieces, particularly those prone to rust, keep them dry and consider applying a coat of wax or oil to seal out moisture.

When dealing with heavily tarnished items, take care not to over-polish, which can strip away the original finish and detail. Sometimes, a little tarnish can add to the antique's charm, so find a balance that maintains the piece's authenticity while keeping it presentable.

PRO TIP

Store metal items in a cool, dry place to prevent tarnish and rust. Use silica gel packs to control moisture levels.

To clean an antique chandelier, turn off the power and lay down a soft towel to catch dust. Gently wipe the crystals with a microfiber cloth damped in a mild dish soap solution. For the metal, stick to a dry cloth to avoid tarnishing. The key is to work section by section.

PRESERVING PORCELAIN AND CERAMICS: FRAGILE BUT DURABLE

Porcelain and ceramic items can be quite durable but still need careful handling. Always support these pieces from the base, not handles or rims, to avoid breakage. Clean them with warm water and a soft cloth, avoiding abrasive cleaners that can scratch the surface or damage glazes. For stubborn dirt, a mild detergent can be used, but make sure to rinse thoroughly to prevent residue buildup.

Repairing minor chips is possible with porcelain repair kits available at craft stores. For significant damage, such as large cracks or missing pieces, it's best to seek professional restoration. Properly displaying these items—using stands or padded surfaces—can prevent accidental knocks and falls.

PRO TIP

Porcelain and ceramics on open display attract dust. You'll want to clean such pieces on a regular basis, before they have a chance to look or feel grimy.

LAMINATE LOGIC: KEEPING YOUR SURFACES SCRATCH-FREE

Preserving and caring for laminate items is all about keeping them clean and preventing damage from moisture or excessive wear. Laminate surfaces, while durable (my favorite personal piece of furniture is my 1970s laminate bullnose dresser), can be prone to scratches and warping if not properly cared for. To preserve them, always use coasters and place mats to protect against spills and heat. Clean with a soft cloth and mild soap or a laminate-safe cleaner—avoid abrasive materials that can dull the finish. Most important, never let water sit on laminate for long, as moisture can seep into seams and cause bubbling or peeling.

If there are any cracks in your piece, you can try a laminate repair paste, also called laminate filler. Choose a color that closely matches your laminate and apply it with a putty knife, smoothing it over the crack. With proper care, laminate pieces can stay looking amazing for decades!

RUGS AND TEXTILES: THE FOUNDATION OF ANTIQUE DECOR

Antique rugs and textiles add texture and warmth to a space but can easily be damaged by foot traffic, spills, and sunlight. Regular vacuuming with a low suction setting helps remove dust without pulling on delicate fibers. Rotate rugs regularly to ensure even wear, especially if they're in high-traffic areas. In case of spills, blot immediately with a clean cloth; don't rub, as this can push the stain deeper into the fibers.

PRO TIP

Sprinkle a little baking soda on your rug before vacuuming to neutralize odors and keep it smelling fresh.

For deep cleaning, it's wise to consult a professional who specializes in antique rugs. If you need to store rugs, roll them (never fold) and keep them in a cool, dry place to prevent creasing and moth damage. Using a rug pad can provide additional protection by cushioning and preventing slippage.

MAKING ANTIQUE GLASS SPARKLE: SIMPLE TIPS FOR CRYSTAL CLARITY

Antique glass pieces, from vases to chandeliers, need a gentle touch. Clean glass items with a mixture of warm water and mild dish soap. Use a soft cloth to wash and dry, avoiding streaks. For hard-to-reach places, a soft-bristled brush can help. If the glass has become cloudy, a soak in a mixture of vinegar and water can often restore clarity. Simply soak the item for a few hours, rinse thoroughly, and dry.

Avoid using abrasive cleaners or pads on antique glass, as these can cause scratches. If the glass is part of a lighting fixture, make sure it's completely cool before cleaning, and avoid getting any electrical components wet.

PRO TIP

Store glass pieces in padded boxes or wrap them in acid-free tissue paper to prevent scratches and chips.

SMALL DECOR ITEMS: CARE TIPS FOR VINTAGE ACCESSORIES

Smaller decor pieces, like picture frames, trinket boxes, and figurines, are often more delicate than they appear. Dust them regularly with a soft cloth to prevent buildup. For metal or glass items, a light polish can enhance their shine. Wooden decor items may benefit from occasional waxing to protect their finish and bring out the wood's natural beauty.

If an item has moving parts, such as a clock or locket, consider having it professionally serviced. These items often contain intricate mechanisms that can wear out or get damaged over time. Proper care will keep them functional and looking beautiful.

PRO TIP

Display small decor items on shelves or in cabinets where they're less likely to be knocked over or damaged.

LEAD PAINT AND SAFE PAINT REMOVAL: PROTECTING YOUR HEALTH AND YOUR PIECES

Older pieces often come with layers of paint that might contain lead, especially if they were painted before 1978. Always test for lead before starting any restoration project. Lead testing kits are available at most hardware stores. If the paint tests positive, it's safer to consult a professional for removal.

For paint stripping, sanding is great for small projects, but always wear a mask to avoid inhaling dust. Chemical strippers are effective for detailed work but should be used with caution. Always work in a well-ventilated area and wear gloves to protect your skin. Once the paint is removed, sanding the surface smooth and applying a fresh coat of primer and paint will give your piece a new lease on life.

PRO TIP

When restoring painted antiques, choose low-VOC or natural paints to keep your home environment healthy.

Recommended Sources

CHAIRISH A treasure trove for vintage and antique finds, Chairish offers a curated collection of furniture, decor, and art from sellers around the globe. It's perfect for scoring one-of-a-kind pieces. This is a go-to resource for me.

1STDIBS Known for its high-end, luxury items, 1stDibs is where designers and collectors go to find rare antiques, vintage furniture, and contemporary art. If you're looking to splurge on a statement piece, this is your website.

AUCTION NINJA This is a great resource for estate sales and online auctions. Auction Ninja offers unique finds at very competitive prices. From antique furniture to quirky collectibles, you can find pretty much anything here. (I know a girl who bought her sofa for $20!)

INVALUABLE An online marketplace for auctions, Invaluable is where you can bid on fine art, antiques, and collectibles. With items sourced from around the world, it's a go-to for discovering timeless pieces. I've gotten a bunch of home decor items here.

H&M HOME H&M Home has a fantastic selection of decor, accents, and everyday essentials for the kitchen and bathroom. Their designs strike a perfect balance between budget-friendly and unique.

ZARA HOME Zara Home offers an extensive collection of furniture and home decor that combines modern style with timeless elegance. It's one of my favorite places for sleek, affordable pieces that have an antique vibe.

EVERYTHING BUT THE HOUSE (EBTH) EBTH specializes in online estate sales, offering everything from furniture and artwork to rare collectibles. It's an affordable way to discover pre-loved items with character.

JAIPUR LIVING Known for their high-quality rugs, Jaipur Living blends traditional craftsmanship with modern design. Their collections are as durable as they are beautiful, making them a great choice for both cozy corners and high-traffic spaces.

ETSY A marketplace for artisans and small businesses, Etsy is where you can find handmade, vintage, and custom items. Many of the sellers are small business owners, so most purchases support a creative entrepreneur.

CURIO BLVD Of course, I have to plug my own brand. At Curio Blvd, we specialize in creating meaningful and sentimental home goods and keepsakes. From our beautifully designed journals that allow your loved ones to record their life story and family history, to our patented keepsake case, designed to preserve your most cherished items and important documents, every piece we create is rooted in the value of sentimentality. At Curio Blvd, we don't just make home goods—we create pieces that hold memories.

Acknowledgments

SO MANY PEOPLE have played a crucial role in bringing this book to life. Maybe it's the hours spent perfecting floor plans, or the countless weekends spent thrifting for the perfect piece of furniture, but I find myself deeply moved as I reflect on this journey.

First and foremost, I want to thank my partner, Mitch, you have been my rock throughout this project. You've spent more weekends doing DIYs than you ever signed up for (I realize that sanding furniture isn't your passion). Whether it's driving hours outside the city on wild thrift adventures or being my emotional support when things get tough, you've been there through it all. I couldn't have done this without you.

To my amazing friends, especially Sara and Nicole, you have stood by me through every twist and turn of my journey as both an author and a decorator. Thank you for always believing in me. Your constant support means everything.

A heartfelt thank-you to my editors, Leslie and Madge, my designer, Sheryl, and my agent, Annie, for taking a leap of faith with me and helping transform this book into something of which I'm incredibly proud. And for enduring my endless barrage of dad jokes and puns—especially the cringe-worthy ones (I couldn't help myself!).

To my parents, you patiently put up with my never-ending furniture rearranging and decor experiments as a kid. Thank you for not kicking me out!

To my fantastic contributors, your spaces have truly captured the timeless beauty of antique design, and I'm so honored to connect with you through these pages.

Finally, to the readers of *City Chic Decor*, my social media followers, and my wonderful clients, thank you for trusting me with your homes and allowing me to inspire you to become your own interior decorators.

Photo & Design Credits

Photo Credits

© 2025 Chelsey Brown front cover & back cover left, 2, 4, 11, 13, 14, 17, 18, 19, 24, 25, 26, 29, 33, 34, 37, 38, 44, 47, 49, 54, 55, 56, 61, 62, 66, 69, 71, 74, 76, 78, 79, 80, 82, 85, 86, 97, 98, 101, 102, 110, 111, 112, 115, 119, 120, 122, 123, 124, 127, 128, 130, 137, 147, 150, 153, 154, 157, 169, 173

Ashi Arizona 6, 42, 43, 72, 73

Martha Behan 38, 141

Nicole Koretsky 8

Paige Kontrafouris 30, 89, 93, 106, 109, 121, 132, 138, 159, 162, 165, 166, 171, 176

Madeline Scalzi 28, 94

Nancy Rodriguez 90, 175

Shannon Dupre DDreps 23, 41, 53, 65, 83, 131, 149

Brigette Muller 51, 58, 99, 105, 116, 135, 161

Designer Credits

Chelsey Brown @chelsey_brown 2, 4, 11, 13, 14, 17, 19, 24, 25, 29, 33, 34, 37, 38, 44, 47, 49, 54, 55, 56, 61, 62, 69, 71, 74, 78, 79, 80, 85, 86, 97, 98, 101, 102, 110, 111, 112, 115, 120, 123, 124, 127, 147, 153, 154, 157, 169

Brigette Muller @hummusbirrd 51, 58, 99, 105, 116, 135, 161

Martha Behan @Marthaishka 6, 38, 42, 43, 72, 73, 141

Jason Saft @stagedtosellhome 23, 41, 53, 65, 83, 131, 149,

Nancy Rodriguez 90, 175

Carly Fuller @mycityapartment 66, 82, 130, 173

Madeline Scalzi @tulipsforthetable 28, 94

Michelle Trinh @chezvudecor back cover middle and right, 26, 76, 119, 122, 128, 150

Paige Kontrafouris @paigekontrafouris 30, 89, 93, 106, 109, 121, 132, 138, 159, 162, 165, 166, 171, 176

Index

First Edition
29 28 27 26 25 5 4 3 2 1

Photo credits on page 180

Published by
Gibbs Smith
570 N. Sportsplex Dr.
Kaysville, Utah 84037
1.800.835.4993 orders
www.gibbs-smith.com

Designed by Sheryl Dickert

Printed and bound in China
Product is made of FSC®-certified and other controlled materials

Library of Congress Control Number: 2024942769
ISBN: 978-1-4236-6595-3